UNTO
THE
HILLS

By Jean Yoder

Cover Photo: Kevin Shank

Christian Light Publications
Harrisonburg, Virginia 22801
1985

First printing 5,000

ISBN: 0-87813-523-5

Lithographed in U.S.A.

CONTENTS

Chapter 1

Calvin

"Teacher, Calvin didn't come today."

"He didn't?" Laura paused to look at Henry. She did not know him too well yet, but she knew he liked to be the first to tell her things. She could see that he had hurried. But why had he thought it so important to tell her that Calvin had not come? Children are sharp. They notice things. Did Henry sense how she felt about Calvin?

Her eyes wandered out to the rising mists that had settled over the hills the night before. The sun shone warmly now, though it had been cool when she had arrived at school that morning. The hills rose tall and mighty about the school, and Laura felt a deep gratefulness to the builder of the school. He must have know what comfort and strength a teacher would get with such a view always before her.

5

She turned to Henry. Just looking at him warmed her heart. His red hair shone, and his freckles, sprinkled so generously over his face, were like so many friendly dots. He was good-natured. True, he poked through his lessons in the most easy, unconcerned way, and if she scolded him, his great blue eyes became dark and burdened. For half a day he would seem to be laboring through great trials. In that time he kept doggedly at his lessons, employing his pencil with great long sighs that seemed to burst from his very heart, while he regarded her with mournful eyes; and she, feeling hardhearted and cruel, was inwardly wrenched with pity.

"Thank you for telling me, Henry." She knew Henry would be glad to visit, but at the moment, she could think of nothing but Calvin. She had known that teaching school would not be easy. And she thought suddenly of her friends and her parents back home. They had been surprised at her decision to teach. Why should she stop a good job in town to teach a little country school? And there had been some shaking of heads and dubious comments.

"You just aren't cut out to be a teacher," one of her friends had told her.

"But I like to work with children," Laura had protested.

Her friend had shaken her head. "I know.

And that is important. But how will you ever make your own decisions? You know how unsure you are of yourself."

"I know," Laura had agreed. "I've always depended so much on my parents."

"And you are an emotional person, Laura. You laugh and cry about the littlest things. How will you manage to keep calm?"

All this Laura knew. And for a time, she had been assailed with doubts. How could she teach if she did not have the qualities of a teacher? But in her heart was a deep longing to do something worthwhile. There was little satisfaction in the paycheck she got every week. Her job in town was just that, a job. There seemed to be nothing meaningful about it. And when they had come and asked if she would consider teaching, she had known this was what she wanted to do.

She had not realized what all teaching would involve. But she was determined to love the children and teach them and mete out punishments when the need arose. *If only*, she sighed to herself, *if only I always knew exactly what to do*. But teaching school had no written directions. It had no dotted lines to follow. Laura had to make the dotted lines. "Please, dear God," she had prayed over and over, "help me do the right things. Make me wise." She knew she was working with immortal souls. And if she caused one of these little one to stumble—what then?

No, she had not expected it to be easy. But she had not reckoned on Calvin, either. She bowed her head there at the desk. She felt ashamed and humbled because she knew she did not feel like a real teacher should when a child is absent. Instead of feeling sorry, a feeling of relief had swept through her.

She knew that with Calvin not in school the day would, in all probability, pass smoothly. She would not have to be on guard every minute . . . strange, how one pupil could affect the whole school and the teacher as well. *If only I could miss Calvin,* and Laura sighed again. But how could she miss her biggest problem, her chief troublemaker?

The next day Calvin was back. And it was a typical day with Calvin in it. As usual he bounded into the schoolhouse. His lunch box clattered onto the shelf. He rushed in to get his mitt.

"Good morning, Calvin."

For a moment Calvin regarded her with his dark eyes, and Laura wondered what he was thinking. But it was hard to tell. Most of the children's faces were as open as a book. They came to her desk and talked. But not Calvin. Inside, Calvin was a boy she did not know. How could she get Calvin to trust her—as a friend?

Now he murmured a greeting and hurried out. Laura bent over the lesson she was preparing. If only Henry and Calvin were a little more alike!

A little later Susie came in. There was dirt on her dress, and she was fighting back tears. By her side, with her arm around her, was Dora, another of the first-grade girls. She was murmuring comforting words to Susie as they came up to Laura's desk, and her little face was full of concern for her little comrade.

"What happened, girls?" Laura asked briskly. She must not show too much sympathy, or Susie would burst into tears.

"We were riding on the wagon and—" Susie gulped, determined not to cry, "— then Calvin gave us a great big push and we dumped out and I scratched my knee and my clean dress is dirty and my mom hoped I could wear this dress tomorrow too." Susie took a deep breath.

"I see. Well, your knee doesn't look too bad. I'll put something on it, and I think we can clean up the dress. Your mother is busy with the baby, isn't she?" Quickly Laura applied the antiseptic. "Dora, would you please tell Calvin to come in?" She was feeling impatient with Calvin. He knew better.

Calvin soon appeared at the door. Several children trailed behind him. Had they come as supporters for Calvin or only as onlookers?

"Go on out and play," she said as she

waved them out. They moved slowly, thoughtfully out the door with one or two looking back, as if expecting Calvin to receive some awful sentence.

Calvin was wearing his innocent look. In fact, he had something of an injured air. Laura walked to the window and looked out. None of the children filled her with exasperation or tried her patience like Calvin. But still, he had a way about him that made her want to laugh when she wanted to be more stern.

"Calvin, why did you push the wagon so hard? You know the little girls cannot guide it around the curves like the older children." Sometimes she wished the little red wagon had never appeared in school. But the children loved it in spite of all the tumbles it caused.

"They wanted me to push them." Calvin stared into space.

If only he would act sorry! But there was no trace of remorse on Calvin's face. It seemed as though it did not matter to him what the teacher would say or do. It was these seeming acts of indifference that baffled her.

"Calvin," Laura paused, "I'm glad you take the time to push the children. They love rides, but you must remember not to push so hard. Why don't you apologize to Susie. Tell her you didn't mean to dump her out."

"Okay, Calvin nodded, acting as unconcerned as possible. He muttered an apology to Susie. And Susie's little face beamed in forgiveness.

"Oh that's all right, Calvin." She smiled radiantly, all her former woes forgotten. Calvin went sheepishly to his desk.

What else could I expect? Laura wondered as she went to ring the bell. If Calvin pushed the wagon, he was sure to push it with all his might. It was the same way when he played ball, or any game. He played hard and he played to win. He was the fastest runner in school, and whenever sides were chosen, Calvin was sure to be the first one chosen. But it was not good for Calvin. And his side usually won. On the rare times it didn't, Calvin could hardly accept losing.

While Laura was taking roll call, she saw Calvin glancing slyly her way. And then she saw his math book and paper, all ready for work as soon as devotions were over.

"Calvin, clear your desk." Laura took a deep breath. She was neither stern enough nor strict enough, else why must she tell him again and again? It was like a tug of war between them, Calvin trying to do everything he could and get by with it. She watched as he put his books back into the desk.

They started to sing, but Calvin's mind was not on singing. He had not combed his hair! Now, he pulled out his comb and combed his black hair. He made little faces and grimaces whenever he encountered a snarl. The smaller children forgot to sing. Fascinated, they watched him. Even with so small an audience, Calvin became quite dramatic. With a flourish and exaggerated motions, his expressions became even more frightful.

"Calvin, don't ever comb your hair during devotions," Laura paused. What could she say to impress or humble him? "Your mind was not on the song we sang, was it?" She glanced down at the hymn they had just finished singing. She realized with a start that *her* mind had not been on the song either. All she had been thinking of was Calvin. One morning he had tied his shoes. Another morning he had brushed his trousers. Why was it so hard for him to sit still and sing? Or sit still and do anything? It was not pleasant having to watch him so closely! It made her feel like a hawk, always ready to pounce down upon him.

She looked out the window. The hills rose calm and peaceful around them. The calm she had felt that morning was gone, and a feeling of frustation was welling up instead. The day had hardly begun. How was she going to cope with Calvin through a whole school term?

After devotions were over, she started with

classes. She had barely finished giving Calvin's class their math assignment until Calvin had his paper out. He was working at a tremendous rate, bending over his paper, furiously scratching away as if his lessons were some terrible beast he must demolish. Laura sighed. Calvin would be finished with his work before Henry had made much of a start. Even now, Henry was just fumbling about in his desk for a piece of paper. If only she could give a portion of Calvin's speed to Henry!

"Remember, Calvin, if your paper isn't neat, you will have to do it over."

Calvin paused. He glanced at Laura and then looked at his paper. He frowned a little. For a minute or two he slowed down. Then he picked up speed again.

Laura went on to other classes. Halfway through a class Calvin slammed his books into his desk. His hand was up, waving impatiently.

"Yes, Calvin," she said when she had finished with the class. She had heard experienced teachers say they did not answer questions when they were having classes, and she tried to practice it too. She knew before asking what he wanted.

"I don't have anything to do."

Laura glanced at the rest of Calvin's class. Henry sat gazing at Calvin thoughtfully. He had managed to do five problems himself

13

There was no envy on Henry's face. Henry was satisfied just as things were. He got out his little pencil sharpener—not that his pencil was broken, but a little sharpening would break the monotony.

"Why don't you get a library book, Calvin?" If only Calvin liked to read! Half bored, he rose and went to the bookshelf. She knew if she didn't give him something to do, he would get into mischief. But what else could she give him to do?

And so the day passed. It was in the last period of the day that Laura discovered Calvin had written some bad words in his book. She stared at them, and a great weight settled upon her heart. It was unmistakenly Calvin's writing, but he would not admit it. Calvin's minor offences were bad enough, but they did not distress her as much as his lies. She could never tell whether he was telling the truth or not, and if a lie served him better, Calvin chose the lie.

"I want you to stay in, Calvin," she told him as the children went out for the last recess. She sat at her desk with bowed head. If only he would tell the truth! The book was new. No one else had used it. She looked at the words again on the clean, fresh page. Words—just words—but they soiled and marred the mind like filthy water would foul a clean cloth.

She looked at Calvin as he sat staring

sullenly out the window. If only she could talk to his parents. How could she inspire him to be good? She could punish him. True, it would put a guard on his actions, but it would also serve to make him more cautious in the future that he would not be found out.

She wanted him to be good because he loved God. And if he cared for her, his teacher, he would want to please her. *But do I really love him?* she asked herself as she sat there. Could Calvin *feel* that she cared about him? She hardly spoke to him except to tell him what he should or should not do. But then he always hurried out at recess. He was not friendly, like Henry.

But she must do something. Tears smarted her eyes. How she dreaded the use of the paddle. She thought of the words of Solomon: "Foolishness is bound in the heart of a child; but the rod of correction shall drive it far from him." She knew it was true. There was nothing as effective as the paddle.

After the unhappy task was done, she talked to Calvin again.

"Saying or writing, or even thinking bad words gives one a dirty mind, Calvin. And you can't wash it out with soap and water, like you would your clothes. Think of the Bible verses you have learned. If those bad words come into your mind, say those verses. See, Calvin, those words make you dirty." Was Calvin thinking about what she

15

was saying? She had no way of knowing. She could not read the expression on his face—was it remorse, resentment, or just plain indifference? She could not tell.

She sat beside him as he copied off a wise saying she wanted him to learn. She watched as he wrote, "Falsehood is cowardice; truth is courage." Laboriously he copied each word. Sudden tears stung her eyes. She looked away. Calvin needed a good teacher, a teacher who was wise and firm and gentle and full of love, one who knew how to cope with his boundless energy, one who knew how to bring out the best in him. And she knew she was not that teacher.

Chapter 2

The Director Brings News

"How would you first graders like to start a song the next time we have singing period?" Laura paused momentarily. She had barely said the words when their little hands flew into the air.

"That's good," she smiled. *If only I always had such a willing spirit,* she thought to herself. She looked wistfully at their shining little faces. The first graders were special. They had an innocence that none of the others had. They trusted their teacher implicitly and completely. She knew if she told them that black was white they would believe her. Hers was an awesome, tremendous responsibility, and a sense of her own weakness swept over her. To Laura it seemed that teaching made her faults stand out so glaringly.

She glanced over the room. The older

children were smiling indulgently at the first graders, and the second graders had assumed an air of experience. Only last year *they* had been in the same shoes, but now they knew what it was all about!

"It will be Marcus and Susie's turn then." Susie's brown eyes sparkled and she smiled in open delight. Marcus tried to look matter-of-fact, but seeing the other children smiling at him, he had to smile too.

"Calvin, please sit up in your desk. And tie your shoes *before* you come to school." Was Calvin improving since his punishment? She was not sure. At least she felt more patient with him.

She was helping Rufus, a little second grader, when she heard a knock at the door. Most of the children looked startled.

"I heard him drive up," Calvin whispered loudly to Henry. Laura hurried to the door. She was startled to see the School Director standing outside. He motioned her to step out and close the door.

"Hello. Is everything going smoothly?" He spoke rapidly, and at Laura's nod, he continued. "There's a new family moving in. I wanted to let you know. They have a girl, Sally. She would be in," the Director paused and scratched his head, "let me see, I think she is in the eighth grade now."

"That will be nice, having another girl. There are just two older girls in school, Betty

18

and Mable—"

"Well . . ." the Director interrupted, then paused. "Sally's folks lived here some years ago." He shook his head. He had the look on his face of wanting to say something and yet not wanting to.

"Well," he began again, cautiously, "make your words count. Remember, we are standing behind you to keep order. We did have some problems with them in the past, but things may have changed."

"Oh," Laura said, thoughtfully. She had learned to appreciate this man. He had an abrupt way about him, and he never wasted words. But beneath his abrupt manner was concern and kindness. *What problems had they had?* She knew the Director had wanted to put her on her guard. Thoughtfully, she turned back toward the schoolroom door.

Betty and Mable were the kind who came to her desk in the mornings to talk. They helped her with extra checking and classes. Their own work was neat and carefully done, and Laura loved to work with them. There was a spirit of comradeship between them. Would Sally . . . what kind of girl was Sally?

Still deep in thought, she opened the door of the classroom. In one glimpse, she took in the whole room. Most of the children were busy. But she was just in time to see Calvin snapping a wad of paper across the room.

"Calvin," Laura's voice was full of disappointment. She glanced at the clock. It was time for recess. "Stay in your desk, Calvin. The rest of you are dismissed."

She watched as they filed out. Picking up a book, she glanced through the next lesson. But she was not thinking of the assignment. Perhaps if Calvin had a little time to think over his actions, he would be sorry.

"Teacher, Marcus pushed me, and I. . . ." Laura looked up to see Christopher standing at her desk. "All I did was I said I want the wagon."

Laura glanced at Calvin sitting glumly at his desk. She looked back at Christopher. Although his parents wanted him to be called by his real name, everyone called him Chriss. He was Mable's little brother, and he was sensitive and easily hurt. The first time he had fallen on the playground, he had screamed. They had rushed to him, sure that he must be seriously hurt. They had helped him up, and Laura was thankful that he could stand. But she could find no external injuries, except a scratched elbow.

"Where does it hurt, Christopher?" she had prodded anxiously. But he only shook his head and sobbed. The tears rolled down his face, faster than ever. He limped back into the schoolhouse. But by the next recess, Chriss had forgotten he had been hurt. Now, whenever Chriss hurt himself, the other boys would look meaningfully at each other. *They* would not cry, no matter how much it hurt. And when Laura heard them denouncing Chriss as a baby and a sissy, even though she could not help having something of the same opinion, she told them that they must never call anyone names.

"All of you have faults," she had told them solemnly. "How would you like it if someone called you, Sloppy Calvin, or . . ." she stopped to think, ". . . or Fat Rufus, or Pokey Henry? That would not be kind, would it?"

"I wouldn't care," Calvin had grinned.

Laura had looked at the faces of the boys. They did not realize how much nicknames could hurt. She did not want any of the children to feel pushed back or inferior. Yet it was so easy to commend those children who excelled, and so easy to speak in a condescending tone to those who were more backward. She had felt exasperated and impatient with Chriss. Now, she wondered if the children had noticed. She knew she must spend more time with Chriss. He was easily discouraged. Whenever his class had something new, Chriss, who had never learned to pay attention and really listen, would declare that it was too hard. He would make an attempt or two, and then, convinced that it was beyond him, he would raise his hand for help. At home he was the youngest. He had been babied and pampered. Now, in school he was finding it difficult to adjust.

"We know," Laura had told the boys, "that Jesus was never unkind. We want to remember that He hears everything we say and do. And we want to practice the Golden Rule. Don't say or do anything to anyone that you would not like said or done to yourself."

"Be brave," she had told Chriss the next time he had fallen. "See, it doesn't really hurt that much does it? Babies cry, but you are not a baby. You are in the second grade, big enough to help the first graders who are younger than you."

But now Christopher was before her, tearful and telling her what Marcus had done. His habit of tattling made him even more unpopular than his habit of crying.

"Look, Christopher," Laura hesitated. It was difficult to define to the small children where to draw the line between talebearing and the need to inform the teacher if an actual wrong was being done. She glanced in Calvin's direction again. He was scowling at Dora who was peeling an orange into the trash can. Laura picked up her Bible on the desk. Over the weekend she had been looking up some references. It was far more impressive to the children when they knew what the Bible said about a certain thing.

"Christopher," she began again quietly,

"do you know what the Bible says about talebearing?"

Christopher looked solemnly at his teacher. "What does it say, Teacher?"

"It says in Leviticus 20 verse 16, 'Thou shalt not go up and down as a talebearer among thy people.'" *Is that too deep for Chriss?* she wondered.

"See, Chriss, usually when you come and tell me things, it is as much your fault as the other person's. Marcus could have come and told me you were selfish and wanted the wagon first. But Marcus didn't come and complain about you. So you see, you are being a talebearer. That causes bad feelings, and you are not practicing the Golden Rule at all."

Chriss looked soberly at Laura. When she was not around, some of the boys called him a tattletale. He did not like that at all.

"But, Chriss," the teacher was talking again, "if someone does something that is wrong, like oh . . . maybe saying bad words, then you come and tell me. Do you understand, Christopher?" The little boy nodded gravely.

After she had dismissed Chriss, Laura turned to Calvin. He was still sitting in the back of the room scowling at Dora, who, not having seen what he had done, had asked him innocently why he did not go out and play.

He stared moodily at his shoes while Laura talked to him. She tried to feel patient and loving, to *show* Calvin that she cared for him, even though he had not behaved. But a counterfeit love, she was finding out, didn't work.

Love must be like the light of a candle— shining without effort or pretense. Children have a way of knowing a teacher's heart. *Will the time ever come that Calvin changes?* she thought. But then she knew that she, too, must change. "Please, God, give me a love for Calvin."

Chapter 3

Head Injury

Moodily, Laura sorted the papers on her desk. She picked up a paper and sighed as she saw the writing. She put it to one side. *Such writing will have to be done over!* She had come early to get some extra work done, but already she could see several figures advancing upon the schoolhouse, like an army that would overtake it with noise and commotion. Yes, that was unmistakably Henry in the lead. He was hurrying, for Henry.

She sighed again as she sat down at the desk. Usually in the fresh new morning she felt ready and eager to begin another day, but now a wave of discouragement and self-pity engulfed her. She stared with unseeing eyes at the desk. Somewhere in the days gone by she had lost her ardor to teach. She had prayed about this—this job of teaching.

Her folks had encouraged her, and Uncle Romans had insisted she board with them since the school was not in her home community. It had all worked out so well. Even though she had doubted her ability to teach, she had felt led to the work that now lay before her. And now, she was wishing it away! She remembered suddenly the visitor she had met in church the week before.

"So you teach school?" the woman had asked.

"Yes," Laura had nodded.

The woman had been full of sympathy. "Well, my sister taught one year and such a time as she had! Yes, indeed, I have a feeling for all you teachers."

"But I like it," Laura had protested. There was something very challenging about it all—the children with their shining faces. *Of course, they do not all shine.* She thought ruefully of Calvin. But they inspired her to go on. Each day you wanted to do your best. At night you would look back and resolve with God's help to make the next day better. It took grit and determination and ever so much patience and love.

But she could not explain all this to the woman, and the visitor had chatted on. It must be tiresome with nothing but books and lessons and children all day. By the time the woman was finished talking, Laura had been left with the vague feeling that she was missing a great deal in life by being "cooped up in a schoolhouse," as the woman described it; and unconsciously, the woman had made her feel as if she were being very noble and self-sacrificing that she should choose to teach.

Thoughtfully, Laura stared at the mountains. Had she let this woman influence her too much?

Laura knew she was easily affected by the moods and words of others, much as she longed to maintain a calm, even, steady temperament.

Now Laura picked up the papers she had planned to check. The top one belonged to Sally, the new student. Sally had been very friendly and talkative at first. It had not taken long to get acquainted. But her work, Laura soon noted, was carelessly done. Had Sally been a younger student, Laura would have easily given the paper back and told her to do it over. But Laura had the feeling Sally would be hurt. Nonetheless, on Friday morning she had handed back the paper.

"This needs to be done over, Sally."

Sally made a little face. "But what is wrong with it?"

"Most of your problems are wrong because you did not divide correctly. See?" Laura helped her do one on the board.

Sally shrugged and went to her seat. She hurried through her paper and went outside while Laura was helping another pupil at the board.

Later, Laura looked over the paper Sally had reworked. Several problems were still wrong, and the work was done in a careless fashion. *So different from Betty and Mable's papers,* she thought.

Annoyed, she had called Sally in and told her to do the problems again.

Now, as she studied Sally's spelling paper, she had more misgivings. It was plain that Sally's accomplishments did not lie in spelling, either.

She looked up to see Henry hurrying up to the schoolhouse. She gave herself a little shake. Here she had been sitting, doing nothing, letting all those precious minutes slip by. She picked up the math book as Henry strode in. She could see at a glance that he had important news to convey.

"Good morning, Henry." It was quite useless to think of getting anything done now. Not with Henry at her elbow.

It was remarkable how Henry's freckles always seemed to be in the mood Henry was in. When Henry was happy, they seemed to shine, adding a glow to his face. When Henry was downcast, those same freckles appeared sad too, making Henry look even more woeful. This morning they stood out with bright importance.

Henry came up to the desk. He had no

time for pleasantries this morning. "Teacher, do you know why Walter is missing?"

"Why, no, I don't. Is he sick?" She had not even noticed that he was not trailing along behind Henry. She took a deep breath. She could not wallow long in self-pity with Henry around. Plainly, Henry was fairly bursting with news about his brother.

"Nooo, he is not sick," Henry spoke with great emphasis on each word. He paused to make his story more suspenseful. Laura, studying his face, could not be sure if something wonderful had happened to Walter, or some tragedy.

"Please tell me," she begged. She had the helpless feeling that she would have to laugh. Henry came closer so he could look squarely into her eyes.

"He fell and knocked a hole in his head." He paused to let the awful import of those words sink in.

Laura gazed at him in silent horror. A hole in his head! Awful pictures came into her mind. Walter lying with a great gaping hole in his head, covered with blood.

Henry was regarding her with great interest.

"Is he, is he in the hospital, Henry?" The accident must have taken place that morning.

Henry shook his head. "No, Mom filled up the hole with ointment."

"With ointment?" Laura shivered. She thought of Henry's mother frantically filling up the hole with gobs of ointment. "But—"

"He's not supposed to move around much."

"He's at home, then?"

"Yes, he's at home. Mom says he has to keep still."

"Well, I should think so." Laura tried to visualize the whole thing. Really, how bad was this? She studied Henry's face. He had moved up even closer. "How far did he fall, Henry?"

"Well, it was kind of high." Henry took a deep breath. The other children were arriving, and they came up to the desk. They listened eagerly as Henry explained what had happened. There were more tales of dreadful accidents, made worse, no doubt, by imagination.

Surely, if Walter is critically hurt, his parents took him to the doctor, Laura reasoned to herself. But it would no doubt be a while before he could come to school. She would send some books home with Henry, once he was able to do some lessons.

"My brother once fell way up this high," little Rufus was saying. He was a second grader but small for his age. Now he smiled sweetly as he recalled his brother's fall.

Laura sat silently, listening to their talk. She had discovered that children's conversations can be very interesting and enlightening. Once again she thought of the visitor she had talked with who thought a school room was dull!

She noticed, then, a big red apple sitting on her math book. So . . . someone had smuggled that up to her desk when she was not looking. There was no telling where it came from. Suddenly she remembered how she felt that morning. Had it really been that morning?

Why did it take so little to cast her down, or to raise her spirits? She felt humbled and ashamed. One should keep faith in any kind of weather. God was always there.

During the noon hour, Laura was astonished to see Walter come walking in. She gazed silently at his head. There was no gaping hole, at least not that she could see. The children greeted him in mild surprise. At recess she came up behind him somewhat stealthily as he stood at the window watching the children playing. She looked over his head. No . . . yes . . . there was a bit of hair, somewhat matted together. And yes, if she looked real closely, she could see where the said hole was supposed to be.

"And how is your head?" she ventured to ask.

Walter shrugged. "It's all right. I'm not supposed to go out though."

And that was that. *Next time*, she told

herself. *Next time Henry tells me something, I'll not be so gullible.*

Chapter 4

Sally

Laura enjoyed her early morning walks to school. There seemed to be a magic in that quiet hour. No, not a magic, a blessing. This morning the clouds hung low. The mountains looked a misty, blue-gray in the distance, and there was a touch of autumn in the air. Autumn was late in coming, loitering as if sorry to see the summer pass on.

What does this day hold in store? Laura wondered. And she thought of Sally. Her problem with Calvin was not resolved. It was always there. But it seemed almost easier to deal with Calvin's out-and-out badness than with Sally's passive rebellion. It was not always what Sally did, but sometimes what she did not do. She seemed to take no interest in her schoolwork at all. When she had to rework a lesson, she complained. And Laura had the feeling that Sally's attitude was affecting Betty and Mable. They no longer came up to her desk to talk. Instead, they hurried out the door.

The day began as usual. Laura was not sure, but was Calvin improving? Or was she getting used to his disturbances? She did not want to get used to it. A teacher should be consistent, keeping order at all times.

She glanced over the room and had an uneasy feeling that the atmosphere was not right. How she wanted to sense the cozy feeling that they were all one big family, in harmony with each other! But she couldn't feel that way this morning. Perhaps it was her imagination. She noticed that Sally kept watching her direction.

When she had the English lesson, she noted with a sinking heart that Sally's paper was neither finished nor neat. "I'm sorry, Sally, but this paper has to be done over. It isn't finished." She handed the paper back. There was no excuse for not having the lesson finished. She would have to take stronger measures with Sally.

Sally shrugged. She glanced meaningfully at Mable and Betty, as if they, too, were in on this. There was a contemptuous, disdainful look in her blue eyes.

Laura felt sudden anger, and hot words trembled on her lips. Words of a former teacher came to her mind then, and she bit her lip. She must not. She looked down at the book in her hands, but she was not seeing the book.

When she had been asked to teach, Laura had gone to a former teacher for advice. "What shall I do," Laura had asked the teacher, "if the children do not behave? What if I can't handle them?"

"Take time to pray, first of all," the teacher had told her. "And do not speak in anger. You can talk to them in front of the whole room. You can shame and scold them, and maybe it will help. But the errant pupil is still in the presence of his peers. He can still feel he may have the support and sympathy of his friends. Scolding and shaming a child does not bring the results you want. It tends to make them resentful."

The teacher had spoken slowly, "If a child misbehaves, send him from the room. This gives him time to think over what he has done. And he may be sorry. Children often act on impulse and regret it later. On the other hand, his offense may have angered you. If so, you are in no condition to admonish him, so take time to pray. Ask God to guide you in the smallest matters. Then go and talk to the child. Show him where he is wrong and punish him if necessary. Alone with you, a child does not feel as brave or daring as he does in the presence of his friends. There is no one around to give him that silent support. Working with him in this way will bring repentance, and it will bring a closeness between you and him.

"Try," the teacher continued, "to put yourself in the child's place. Respect his feelings and he will respect you too. If you can get students to obey you because they love you, and not because they have to, it will make all the difference. Sometimes, of course, an open rebuke is necessary. . . ."

Now, Laura suddenly realized she had reached a crisis. There was Sally with her resentful attitude and Laura had the feeling that at least part of the class sided with her. Sally obviously did not respect her.

Laura went on with the class, but later she could not remember what she had assigned them to do.

At recess, she asked Sally to stay in, although she was not yet sure how to deal with her. It seemed silly to say, "Sally, you must not look at the others when I tell you to do your work over." No, that would not do. Sally's problem was deeper than that. It was an attitude. *How do you change attitudes?*

"Sally," she began, "this paper is not finished, and most of the answers are wrong. So do the whole lesson over." She hesitated before going on. She was not sure how to word what she wanted to say. "Handing in unfinished papers does not show dependability, Sally. And after this, if you hand any in, there will be a punishment, unless there is a good reason for it."

Laura hesitated again. The look on Sally's face was not encouraging. She had never before known how hard it is to talk to someone who is irresponsible and distant. She could say words, but they seemed meaningless. "You would feel so much better, Sally, if you would take an interest in your work. Strive to do your best. Any task you start is worth finishing and worth finishing well."

"Mom says she can't see why it is so important that we learn this stuff anyway." Sally tossed her head. "At the school we came from we had lots more time to read and do other things."

"But it is important, Sally. And if you don't learn now, it will be your loss."

Sally shrugged. She took the paper to her desk and Laura checked some papers. How could she get Sally to do better work if her mother did not consider her schoolwork important? Laura felt defeated.

When Sally had her paper finished, Laura saw with relief that it was improved.

At the next recess, as Laura went out to help the children play, she came upon the girls standing at the corner of the schoolhouse. They were whispering together. At the sight of Laura they stopped. "Why aren't you playing, girls?" She looked at them inquiringly.

"We don't want to play," said Sally. "I'm tired of playing ball." The others nodded in agreement. But Laura knew. Betty and Mable had always liked to play ball before Sally came.

Laura hesitated, and the girls, taking advantage of the moment, turned and went back into the schoolhouse. Laura made her way out to the playground. The girls would go in and whisper, and that was not good. If she made them play, they would resent it. What should she do? Heavy-hearted, she joined the other children.

While she played, Laura found herself thinking. *I don't want to confront the older girls. I want them to enjoy me as a friend.* Laura decided at least to put off any confrontation till later.

But that evening at the supper table, Laura found it hard to eat.

"Is everything going all right in school?" Aunt Rachel asked. She passed the platter of fried chicken again.

Laura looked down at her plate. She had a longing to pour out her troubles, but deep down was a stronger fear of admitting she had problems. It seemed like admitting failure.

She managed to change the subject, but underneath, she felt a rising resentment at the problems she knew she was having and also at herself for not admitting them to others.

"The first graders are planning to lead in singing next time." Laura speared two peas on her fork. They had just a taste of butter.

"Well, that is good," Uncle Roman nodded. He was a good singer himself. "The sooner they learn, the better."

"They are looking forward to it," Laura said.

As soon as the supper dishes were done, she hurried to her room.

The rest of that week passed. The girls were distant, almost like strangers when they were around her. And they avoided her when they could.

On Sunday, after the morning service, Betty's mother came upon Laura, who was standing apart from the others on the porch. She was staring with unseeing eyes at some of the children who were gathered in the yard. "Well, Laura, how are you getting along?"

Laura turned swiftly. She looked at the kind, friendly woman.

"Well," she began hesitantly, "I am having some problems. . . ."

"We suspected as much," Betty's mother nodded.

"You did?" Laura looked surprised.

"Yes. You see, Betty is quite frank. I imagine this started when Sally came to school?"

"Yes," Laura nodded. Last night she had been too proud to tell her troubles to Uncle Romans. She realized this now since the morning message. Now, as her eyes searched the woman's face, she felt instinctively that here was someone who would understand.

"Sally's folks used to live here some years ago. Then they moved, and now they are back again. But I feel you should know," Betty's mother moved closer and her voice was low and earnest, "that Sally needs help. Her mother has let her have her own way all these years, and it is just too bad. Poor Sally is not really to blame is she?" The woman paused. "Of course there were problems before they moved away. And I had hoped things had changed when they came back again. But anyway, the trouble with the girls, Laura, is simply that Sally cannot stand it when you correct her. She talks about you to the other girls. We told Betty if we find out she does not behave, she will be punished. A teacher must have the respect of her pupils. I am afraid if this goes on it will lead to more problems."

"What should I do?" Laura clasped her hands together.

"Well, the next time you need to call Sally down, I would give her a punishment. You may have trouble, but we are standing behind you. Sally needs a lot of love, but she also needs discipline. You know, Laura, when you and I were children, it gave us a feeling of, oh, what would you call it—security? I think that's the word to express it—when our parents punished us and saw to it that we obeyed the rules. Somehow, it was something to lean on. It made us secure in the knowledge that they loved us."

Laura nodded slowly. She was seeing why the trouble had only been mounting. Her failure to deal openly with Sally's attitude was only letting the resentment grow more.

"I am afraid I am confusing you," Betty's mother said, but Laura shook her head.

"No, please go on."

"Well, if I can explain what I mean," the little woman continued. "Sally does not get that security. And I wonder sometimes if she feels inferior and tries to hide her feelings by acting as she does."

Laura thought of Sally's behavior. Sally feel inferior? It seemed impossible.

"I taught school for a number of years, so I know what you are going through."

"Really?" Laura said, surprised.

"Yes, I taught in my home community. I had a book that helped me to understand children. They all come from different homes. They have different needs. Some children crave attention, and some are shy. You have to draw them out. So I tried to look at them in a special way. You know, children are little people. They have their problems which are very real and agonizing to them." Betty's mother paused. "I did not mean to talk so much. . . ."

"Please go on," Laura said eagerly. "It helps so much to talk to someone who has experience."

"Well, I always felt that way too," the woman smiled warmly. "So I just want to say again, don't let the problems get you down." She stopped, thoughtful. "You know," she continued softly to Laura, "it was when the going was the hardest that I learned how little I am, and how great God is. When everything goes well, we are apt to depend on our own strength. We don't really grow then, do we?" She smiled faintly. "But when the stormclouds darken our lives, it is then we grow stronger."

"Yes, that is true." Laura had never thought of it that way, but it was so.

"Now you let us know if we can help you in any way. I see the others are getting ready to go, so I had better get my wraps too."

"Thank you so much," Laura said gratefully as the kindly little woman turned to go. Betty's mother had given her fresh courage. She had never thought of one's troubles as being in any way helpful, but she knew it must be so. She had much to think about as she walked slowly to Uncle Romans.

That evening she opened up to her uncle

and aunt.

"That is all very well," Uncle Roman agreed. "Scolding and shaming children is the human way, the easiest way. It takes much prayer, time, and effort when you work with children. And you need to make Sally obey. If she does not want to play, give her lessons to do."

Laura nodded. If only she had confided sooner in them. She still had that heavy weight of responsibility and the problems facing her, but now at least she was not alone.

"Sally needs your love," Uncle Roman was saying, "and if you knew everything, maybe you'd find out that Betty and Mable aren't so happy either. They liked you to begin with. Then Sally came and they wanted to be friends with her, too. Now they are in a rather hard place."

"Yes," agreed Aunt Rachel. "I can imagine how it is with the girls. In order to be Sally's friends, they have to side with her. It would be better if they would help Sally, but Sally has always been a leader, and they likely go along with her." Aunt Rachel paused. "Did you tell Betty's mother how the girls are acting?"

"No, not really. We were busy talking and I didn't think of it. Betty doesn't really do anything. She just goes along with the others."

"It is very hard for children that age to stand alone. There's a fear of being different and being laughed at. It is so important to belong, to be in the same peer group. They are at a very difficult age. I remember the trying times I had," Aunt Rachel added.

"I know. But it is so easy to forget sometimes."

"Well, it is easy to magnify our troubles too," Uncle Roman said quietly. "Something happens and we imagine the worst. Sometimes it turns out to be nothing at all, and other times it is just the opposite. The best thing is to be prepared at all times," Uncle Roman smiled. "The trouble is, problems often come when you least expect them."

"That is true," Laura agreed. "And things never, or hardly ever, turn out like you expect them too—not in school anyway."

Chapter 5

Spanking

"Teacher, I'm going to sing a song we always sing."

Laura looked up. Susie had not bothered to take off her wraps. She stood excitedly before her, her lunch box in one hand and a book in the other. Her brown eyes shone with eagerness and her little face beamed with happiness.

Laura had forgotten. This was the day the first graders were going to sing. "What song are you planning to sing, Susie?"

"It is, 'What a Friend We Have in Jesus.'" Susie set her lunch box down and clasped her hands together. "Is it time for the bell?"

Laura glanced at the clock. "In a little while, Susie." Susie hurried out to the coat room. When Laura went to ring the bell, Susie was sitting in her desk, her songbook open to the right page.

Laura winced. There was something about Susie's eager, earnest little face that moved her. All through roll call she was conscious of Susie, waiting with her open songbook, ready to begin her first song.

"All right, Susie, what is the number?" Marcus had not fully decided what he would sing. The other children smiled knowingly, while the rest of the first grade stared wonderingly at Susie. Susie gave out her number. Laura paged quickly. She wanted to be ready to help Susie the minute she started, just in case she forgot the tune.

But before she could utter a sound, Susie started in. She sang the first line in her high-pitched, singsong little voice. Quickly Laura chimed in. It took a bit to start the second line on the right pitch, but finally they were off.

Fearfully, Laura glanced at Susie. Even Calvin huddled miserably in his seat and turned red if he failed to start a song correctly. "It is nothing to be ashamed of," Laura had told them many times. "Everyone makes mistakes, and making a mistake in starting a song is nothing bad. You shout around on the playground. You don't care when people hear you then."

Now, she expected to see Susie in tears. But as she looked, she saw Susie was sitting up, straight as a ramrod. Her eyes shone with happiness. In the excitement of having started the song, she had forgotten to go on and sing. But she was smiling with joy. The other first graders were regarding her with wondering, admiring eyes. Susie had started a song!

Laura looked down at her songbook. She had the sudden, terrible desire to laugh. She had expected to see the girl in tears, now Susie did not even realize. . . . She kept hearing Susie's piping little voice, seeing her shining little face. Laura pinched herself. It was not funny. If the children had laughed she would have rebuked them with a look. Now she, the teacher, was sitting there unable to sing, shaking with suppressed laughter. She tried to concentrate on the deep, meaningful words of the song. She felt helpless, as she choked into her handkerchief. But finally, at the end of the verse, she was able to sing again in a jerky, trembly voice. But she did not look up until the song was ended.

"Now, Marcus, what is your song?" Laura felt composed again. Marcus gave out his number. Then he sat and stared open-mouthed at Laura.

"Can you start it, Marcus?" she prodded, gently.

Marcus looked at the song. Then he looked at Laura again. He had sung the song at home. But now when he opened his mouth, no sound came out.

Softly, encouragingly, Laura began the song, and immediately Marcus joined in.

As Laura began the classes, she puzzled over the morning. It was like Uncle Roman said, almost nothing turned out like you expect. She had felt sure that Marcus would be able to start his song. He was a good little singer. He could carry a tune and he had a strong voice. But she had been fearful for Susie. For effort, Susie should certainly have an A.

As Laura walked back to answer a question, she saw a bit of paper on the floor beside Mable's desk. "To Mable," she read silently. She put it into her pocket. What did this mean? Writing notes was forbidden. A feeling of foreboding swept over her.

So far this week had gone quite well. Laura took time to answer a few more questions. Then she went to the desk and unfolded the little note. "Dear Mable," she read. "Won't the teacher be upset when she sees what we plan to do at recess? Why does she pick on us and let the boys go?"

There was a rustling of papers, and Laura looked up. Karl had upset his notebook, and papers were strewn all about him on the floor. He smiled a cheerful, apologetic little smile as he saw Laura's eye upon him. Then he busied himself to pick them up.

Laura glanced down at the note. There

was more, but she looked at the signature and stuffed it into her pocket. It had been signed, "Sallie." *Spelled with an* ie *at that!* She felt disgusted and angry. What had she done to make the girls think she favored the boys? She thought swiftly over the past days. She had seen to it that the girls stayed with the whole group, aiming to keep them occupied so that they had no chance to go off by themselves. She knew she had made a mistake in leaving them to themselves. Apparently Sally resented this. Did Sally really feel inferior? It hardly seemed possible. And then Laura suddenly thought, *when Sally has the girls to herself, she feels she has the upper hand. But under my eye, Sally has to conform. Is that why she feels inferior?*

Laura could not bring herself to feel loving towards Sally. All Sally's faults tumbled about in her mind. "Sally has always been something of a leader," Betty's mother had said. *Why does Sally feel she must be in the lead?*

Laura glanced at the clock. It was a little early, but no matter, she dismissed for recess.

"Sally, you and Mable may stay in your seats."

Sally gave Harvey a knowing look. Whatever Harvey felt he hid behind a noncommittal expression, and Laura felt a surge of anger. She watched Harvey as he went out.

He was a quiet, studious boy in the seventh grade. There was something about him that stood out. He never argued, never fussed. He did his lessons to the best of his ability. He played with the others at recess, but it was not the gay, happy play of youth. Even when they played ball, Harvey was serious. He was so well-behaved that Laura ached sometimes. She wanted him to be good, but she wanted him to have the happy, carefree times that children should have, too. He and Sally were *so* opposite!

The small children cast curious glances at Mable and Sally. Everyone went out except Henry. He came up to her desk importantly. For once, Laura felt impatient with him. Whatever he had to say could be said at another time!

"Teacher," he came closer. "Can we eat candy through school?"

Laura felt more annoyed than ever. "Of course not, Henry. What ever gave you such an idea?"

"Oh, I just wondered." Henry paused mysteriously. Laura's impatience was becoming evident.

"Were you?" Laura was suddenly suspicious. "Were you eating some, Henry?" If only he would hurry and come out with it. She glanced at Mable and Sally. Mable looked uncomfortable, but Sally was staring out the window.

"No, I wasn't eating candy." Henry paused.

"Well, who was eating candy, Henry?"

"Calvin has a bag in his desk."

"And he eats it in schooltime?"

"He eats it now and then."

Laura sighed deeply. What should she do first?

"Sally," and there was an ominous tone in Laura's voice. "Go out to the closet."

How glad she was for the broom closet. It was large and roomy enough to hold one or two erring pupils and the teacher. And really, it was the only place where anyone could have any privacy. What problems and conspiracies had not been dissolved in that little room! It was the lowest a child could sink if he heard those words of doom, "Go out to the broom closet!"

But Sally appeared unmoved. Holding her head high, she went out of the room to the dreaded closet.

Laura took the note out of her pocket and read it again. She looked at Mable, and she could see Mable looked miserable.

"Mable, when did Sally give you this note?" Laura was upset, and in her agitation, she had forgotten to take time to meditate and pray. Outside, the mountains rose tall and majestic, but Laura did not think of them.

Mable twisted her hankie. "She, she just

gave it to me this morning." This was the first time Mable had had to stay in, and her face said clearly she was feeling it deeply.

"And where is the one you wrote her?" Laura's voice was low and dreadful.

Mable looked up, surprised. "I didn't write any."

"Then you haven't been writing notes before?" Laura's voice sounded normal again.

"No . . ." Mable hesitated. Laura looked so stern. "I . . . I," she faltered, "I was going to answer that one, but I hadn't yet." Two tears fell on the desk.

Laura bit her lip. After all, Mable was not to blame. She was honest about it. She would not have had to admit that she had intended to answer this one.

"I'm glad you did not write any, Mable. You girls know it is against the rules." She dismissed Mable who was still tearfully wringing her hankie.

Now, what next? Surely she would have seen if Calvin had been eating candy! Henry had a big imagination. She walked to Calvin's desk. She would check to make sure. She stooped down and peered into its depths. There, before her startled eyes she saw it—not one or two pieces, but a whole bagful. Stunned, she stared at the label, *Gum Drops*. Even the label seemed bold and daring. How had Calvin smuggled this in without her knowing?

Suddenly she felt almost triumphant. For once, Calvin had been caught red-handed. This time she had proof. But what should she do first? Sally was in the closet. Calvin was outside playing. No, it would not hurt Sally to sit awhile in the closet.

Still feeling mighty and terrible, she called Calvin in. He eyed his teacher curiously. And Laura noted he was looking as innocent as possible. "Calvin, have you been eating candy through classes?" She watched him covertly, sure that he would deny it. But she knew the truth this time no matter what he would say. And he would not get by with it either!

But Calvin looked unabashed. He did not hesitate at all. "I've been eating for my cold."

"Your cold?" She stared at him in disbelief.

He nodded. He coughed. It was a poor excuse of a cough, but he tried. "See, every now and then my throat tickles."

Laura turned suddenly away. All that she had built up in her mind had been swept away, and now she felt helpless. How could Calvin turn the tables so quickly? She had felt so stern, and now she felt she must laugh. "Look, Calvin," she tried to keep her voice steady. "I did not know you even had a cold. But bring your candy up to my desk, and when you have a cold, I will give you something for your throat."

Calvin nodded cheerfully. He went to his desk and scooped up the pieces that had fallen out of the bag. He deposited them all in the bag and brought it up to her. "Thank you, Calvin. Remember, no eating candy through classes."

She no longer felt mighty and terrible. She felt small and weak and helpless. She had been so sure of what Calvin would say. True, his alibi had seemed ridiculous. His cold was no doubt weeks old and quite worn out. But at least he had had a alibi. Laura stared at the mountains. A teacher must *never, never* jump to conclusions!

Then she remembered Sally out in the broom closet and her feeling of frustration and anger returned. "Never talk to a child when you are angry." The words sounded in her mind like a bell. What had she been thinking of when she talked with Mable and Calvin? She had not been exactly angry, but neither had she been calm. She had been frustrated and upset. She had not taken time to pray. And now, when she thought of Sally, she did not want to be kind and gentle. She could not feel any love in her heart just then, only a desire to give her a good punishment.

She stared with troubled eyes at the distant mountains. Calm, peaceful they were, and they rebuked her silently, for they spoke so eloquently of their Maker who had a boundless love for all His creatures. *Please God, help me love Sally. Please God, I do not feel any love for her at all.*

Bits of advice came into her mind. When a child is most unloving, then he needs the most love. . . . When you punish a child, it should hurt you to do it. But into her mind kept coming all the things Sally had done. She struggled with her feelings. She must do something. Sally was still in the closet. *Please God, help me. Don't let me be rash. Oh, help me to love Sally.* She sat with bowed head at the desk.

The closet door was closed. Laura opened it quietly. Sally was seated on a box. She looked sullenly at Laura.

"Sally, here is a note I found." Laura noted that Sally looked a little startled. She went on, "You know that writing notes is not allowed. When did you write this one, Sally?"

Sally looked down. "I don't remember."

"You don't remember, Sally?"

Sally looked up. There was that in Laura's voice that compelled her to look at her. She colored slightly as she met Laura's eyes.

"Don't you remember writing the note this morning?"

Sally shrugged. She stared at the floor.

Laura, looking at the downcast countenance of her student, felt her anger draining away. There was something pathetic about Sally. She had tried to fix her hair in an attractive way, but she had only succeeded in making herself look frowsy. Her dress had been made as stylish as possible. Laura knew that Sally's mother sewed Sally's clothes. Sally's mother had done all she could to make her daughter attractive outwardly . . . but what about the inside?

Laura knew she could not blame Sally. How could she be otherwise, if she had never been taught to be respectful and obedient? What was it Betty's mother had said? "Sally's mother has always let Sally do as she pleased."

An awesome feeling swept over Laura. Here was an immortal soul. Laura had an awesome responsibility, and in that moment Larua knew she did love Sally. It swept over her in an overwhelming force. "Thank You," she prayed silently.

"Sally, I must punish you. You broke the rules, and you were not respectful." Laura went on to mention the things that Sally had done. Then she reached with trembling hands for the paddle. She knew, somehow, that she must use it. "Only as a last resort for the big students," a teacher had told her. She had talked to Sally and had kept her in, but now she must do more.

Sally stared mutely at the teacher. She watched as Laura brushed the tears from her eyes, and she submitted quietly to her punishment.

The rest of the day passed quietly. That evening, as Laura gathered up her books to go home, she glanced around the room and her eyes lighted on Susie's desk. Was it only that morning that Susie had started her song? It seemed like years ago. Wearily Laura picked up her books. She felt drained. It had been a long day.

Chapter 6

Two Mothers

"We heard our Mable had to stay in at recess."

So this was Mable and Christopher's mother. Laura had seen her before, but they had not exchanged more than a few words together. She had noticed she wore a habitually worried expression. Laura was glad that she had cared enough to come and talk to her. She had probably been hearing things too. There was nothing as heartening to a teacher, Laura had found, as a good, understanding talk with a parent.

Laura looked about the room. It was what Uncle Roman had called an Apple Bee. The community had come together to cut up apples to make apple butter. Fortunately, she and Mable's mother were at one end of the room, quite by themselves, just right for a little talk.

"Yes," Laura said, answering her question. "But I—" She got no further. Mable's mother was talking again.

"The way Mable said, she didn't even do anything, and then Christopher came home and said that Mable had to stay in at recess, and Mable was in tears too when she got home."

"The way it was, I kept her in to find out—"

"Now we want our children to behave, of course. But Mable has always gotten along fine with her teachers before, and her conduct was good too. And Mable is very sensitive." The little woman dabbed at her nose.

"Oh," Laura stammered. She remembered that day so well. She knew she had been hasty and abrupt. If only she could tell this mother how it had been. "I did not keep her in to punish her. I wanted to find out—"

"Yes, I know. Mable said she was blamed for passing notes. But it was Sally. But Sally has to have friends too."

"Of course. I—"

"And Christopher says some of the boys aren't nice to him. He feels they don't like him."

Laura swallowed. What should she say? What could she say? Christopher was overly sensitive, so easily hurt.

"And then the children say you aren't out on the playground much."

59

"I try to be as much as I can but—"

"Now I always think a teacher should be out on the playground with the children. Then she can see what is going on."

Laura looked down at her bowl of apples. She knew it was true. She knew she should spend more time on the playground with the children. And had this good bit of admonishment come from Uncle Romans, or Betty's mother, who had such a kind and understanding way about her, Laura would have been glad for it. As it was, she was feeling guilty and ashamed. And this advice, coming on top of everything, seemed a little too much. Laura felt a feeling of resentment rising within her, and the thought crossed her mind that perhaps if this lady hadn't babied Christopher so much there wouldn't be so many problems.

"Yes, of course," she agreed. She tried to stifle the unkind feeling that kept rising in her heart. It was wrong to feel so. A teacher should be open to criticism, ready to accept the well-meaning advice she was given, even if it was not given in the most tactful way.

"Well, we want to know it, of course, if our children do not behave. But they have feelings, too."

"Yes, yes, I know." Laura nodded. She felt small, shorn of all her self-confidence. The little woman moved off to get more apples. Laura did not look up when someone came and sat beside her. But she knew it was not Mable and Christopher's mother. She had worn a brown dress. This one was blue. No doubt every one there was wondering why she had ever attempted to teach school in the first place.

"This will make a nice mess of apple butter."

"Yes, quite." She should say something more, but she could not think of a single thing to say.

"It is a nice evening, but a little on the cool side." The speaker had a kind voice.

"Yes, it is indeed. Very nice." She must say something more. It was kind of this person to come and talk. If only she could be alone to get out in the fresh night and gaze at the hills. They would be rising, quiet and majestic to the heavens. They would give her courage again.

By now the lady in blue had moved off for more apples, and this time she chose another place to sit. Laura cut up apples, one by one, and the whole evening stretched out endlessly before her.

"Ah, there you are!"

Laura looked up in surprise. She knew the woman, but her name . . . what was it?

"I'm Dora's mother, Esther. Remember? We met before, but I can imagine meeting so many parents you find it hard to remember everyone."

61

"That's right," Laura said cautiously. But Dora's mother was beaming with friendliness. She sat beside Laura in a cozy, friendly way.

"You know," she began, and there was a worried, anxious look on her face. "I'm just so worried about Dora."

For a moment, Laura's heart seemed to stand still. Dora . . . had something happened to her? Maybe she had an incurable disease! Anxiously she looked at her mother. She was frowning anxiously as she cut up the apples.

There was no one like Dora. She was so sweet and unselfish that Laura felt sometimes she could not stand it—like the time she had a little pack of potato chips in her lunch. Potato chips were a rare treat for Dora. Her mother had put them in as a surprise for her.

"Umm. May I have one?" asked one little girl.

"They look so good," said another. Generously, Dora passed the little pack around. And when it came back to Dora, there were only a few bits and crumbs left.

"Don't ask," Laura told the children later, when she found out what had happened. "It is not polite to ask or hint for things." It was Dora who waited till last, whether they were playing jump rope, or lining up for drinks. All this was trooping through Laura's mind as she gazed anxiously at Dora's mother.

"Please tell me," she begged.

"It's this way," Esther began in a confidential way, but still in that worried tone. "Dora says that they, the first graders, have to take turns to sing, and she can hardly wait till her turn comes. You know, Susie sang, and Dora said she did just wonderful." Esther took a deep breath before going on. "But what I am so worried about, Dora can hardly wait for her turn, but she can't even carry a tune!" Esther's sentence ended in a kind of wail. She looked at Laura with despairing eyes. "I just did not know should I encourage her or discourage her." She stopped and looked hopefully at Laura. "I knew you would not make her sing if she couldn't."

"Of course." Laura was so relieved she felt like laughing. "I mean, yes, she won't have to sing if she doesn't want to. Some of the others can't carry a tune either. But we help them right away, and it gives them a feeling of taking part anyway."

"Then you don't think I need to be anxious about it?"

"Oh, no. Not at all."

"Well, I am so relieved." Esther took a deep breath. We do want her to do her work right and take part in everything she should. Then I should just go ahead and encourage her?"

63

"Oh, yes. That helps. That helps a lot." Laura took a deep breath. A half hour ago, she was feeling shamed and miserable. Now, Dora's mother was making her feel quite wise and experienced.

"You know, Dora loves school. She just talks and talks about it. She used to be kind of, oh, scared like of the other students. But now she comes home and tells me what all good times they have. And she coaxes me to come to school, and I am intending to one of these days." Esther paused for breath. She cut up apples vigorously. "Now do tell me about school. I think the children do such interesting things."

"Indeed they do," Laura agreed warmly. She glanced around the room. At the other end she saw Mable's mother, still with that worried expression on her face. She turned to Dora's mother and started to relate something that had happened that day, and Esther listened avidly. Their conversation drifted to other topics.

Laura looked up in surprise when Uncle Roman came sometime later and asked if she was ready to go home. The evening had flown!

Later, in the quiet of her room, Laura thought over the evening. Though her encounter with Chriss and Mable's mother had not been pleasant, she knew it had been good for her. If all mothers were like Dora's mother, there would be a danger that she would become overconfident. And the difference between Dora and Chriss—Chriss who felt pushed back and was so easily hurt; Dora who loved school, who gave so generously, never thinking of herself. What made them so different? And she thought of the two mothers.

She must remember that in her little kingdom, she had children with all kinds of different feelings, different training, different homes. *But I am glad,* she thought, *for mothers like Esther, even if they do worry needlessly.*

Chapter 7

Frustration

With a thankful heart, Laura noticed that Sally was doing better. The punishment had not been in vain. And that warm feeling for Sally was still there in her heart. She knew God had given it to her. For though Sally was doing better, she avoided her, as did Mabel and Betty. They seemed uncomfortable in her presence.

Laura tried to ignore it. She called on them to do the little errands they had always enjoyed doing for her. She talked to them, hoping that eventually the "thaw" would come.

She longed to help Sally. The more she studied her student, the more she realized that some of the things Sally did were a cover-up to hide her real self. She would laugh and talk noisily, looking around for attention. Why did Sally want attention? Did it give her a feeling of security, make her feel less inferior? Betty was quite the opposite. She was quiet and well-mannered, with a certain self-reliance that made her seem older than her years. As for Mable, Laura took great care not to hurt her sensitive pupil. She knew that girls Mable's age are sensitive.

As Laura looked about the room that morning, she realized that she was learning many things from her students. While she taught them from books, they were teaching her, but so unconsciously, those little lessons from the heart. Where but in the heart of a child could one find such generosity? If someone needed a pencil, half a dozen hands would fly into the air. "Here's mine! I've an extra one. I have a *new* one. This one's just sharpened."

Once when Laura had needed a pencil, she could hardly decide whom to borrow from. The one chosen would surely gloat while the rest would look crestfallen. She had finally chosen the one whose hand she saw first in the air.

But generosity was not the only virture present in her little kingdom. Each student made a contribution. There was Dora who was so unselfish. Susie who verily would try to conquer the unconquerable.

"Please, God, make me as willing and unselfish as my little girls."

There was patient little Rufus, who toiled on uncomplainingly.

"Please, God, make me patient and meek."

There was Henry, the embodiment of friendliness and goodwill. There was Karl, generous, cheerful in adversity. Harvey who was so quietly good, so sweet and patient with the little children. The list went on.

And Sally? But Laura knew she was learning through Sally too. She was beginning to see what all a child misses and lacks by not getting the right kind of love and discipline at home.

She was not sure what she received from Calvin, unless it was the opportunity to develop patience. There was no one, just no one, who tried her patience like Calvin. He had good qualities if only he would use them right. He was certainly not lazy. Whatever he did, he did with all his might.

As the children went out to recess. Laura followed them. But seeing that the oldest girls had failed to come out, she went inside again. As she stepped into the entry, she heard Mable say, "Mom says Laura is just too particular."

The girls, unaware that Laura had come in, moved on out the door and Laura returned slowly to her desk. She knew she should not let the remark hurt her. But it did, nonetheless. How did the parents expect her to teach, keep order, and have the respect of her students if they talked about her? And this, coming from Mable's mother, called up the old struggle again against the feeling of resentment, the feeling that the mother, never having taught school, had no idea what it was like or what problems a teacher had.

The windows were open, and Laura suddenly realized by the sounds on the outside that not all was well on the playground. She hurried out. She took in the situation in one glance. Calvin was guarding first base. He was sure it had been an out. The opposite side was sure it wasn't.

"Aw, come on. Pitch the ball." It was good-natured Henry on the pitcher's mound. "Tie goes to the runner."

The others nodded. But Calvin glowered darkly. He clung to the ball stubbornly.

"Come into the schoolhouse, Calvin," Laura said quietly. As Laura returned to the schoolhouse with Calvin, she noticed that Mable, Betty, and Sally were sitting under one of the trees. They had not been helping to play at all. Her heart sank, and she knew she had failed again. Had she been out on the playground, instead of brooding over the remark she had heard, she would have avoided these two problems. Now, she must deal with the girls and with Calvin, and all the while she should be out on the playground!

Calvin marched into the schoolhouse. His eyes blazed. For a moment Laura remained on the steps. She looked at the grandeur of the hills. In their sheltering coves were dainty mountain flowers and cool grass. There would be peace and quiet with the rippling, musical sound of the brook as the water tumbled over the rocks. She wondered suddenly if King David in the Bible had not longed sometimes to be a simple shepherd boy again instead of being king over all the people. And it seemed to her as she stood there, that she had a mountain before her, a mountain she had to conquer. With a silent plea for help, she followed Calvin inside.

She went to her desk and picking up her Bible, started paging through the Book of Proverbs. Where was it, the verse about the man who could govern his spirit being better than he that takes a city? She glanced at Calvin. The dark, scowling look was disappearing. At least Calvin did not stay angry.

When she had found the verse, she showed him. "See, Calvin, how little a man is who cannot control his temper? It takes far more willpower and strenth to be quiet when we feel like raging. And every time you are quiet and control your temper, you get that much stronger."

"Dad loses his temper."

"But, Calvin, I believe if you would ask him, he would say he is sorry that he does."

Calvin stared moodily at the wall. "There goes a spider," he said suddenly.

Laura sighed. Did her words just roll off him like water off a duck? Here he was thinking of spiders.

"Well, I'll let you kill it, Calvin." She shivered as he whacked the spider with relish.

"And being a good loser, Calvin, is much more important than winning the game." She handed him the paper. She had a futile, useless feeling. Did other teachers talk as much as she did and see as few results? "Write this the rest of recess."

Now for the girls. She must find out why they had not been playing with the rest of the children.

She questioned them, but they said little. They shrugged their shoulders and looked down. They didn't know why they had not helped.

Laura talked to the girls. They should be friends with all the girls. Being the oldest was no reason for them to pair off by themselves. She glanced at the clock. It was time to ring the bell. After this, Laura decided, she would have to give the girls some punishment if they did not stay with the group and play. And in the back of her mind was the realization that Mable's mother might be upset again. It was not a pleasant thought.

After school was dismissed that day. Laura started to check papers. The autumn sun shone warmly against the window, and a bee buzzed about trying to find its way out again.

She glanced up at the window. The leaves were a riot of colors, making the countryside alive with their beauty. Suddenly, Laura laid down her pencil. She did not want to check papers. She did not want to prepare lessons. She was tired of talking. And she had talked so much that day! She thought of Calvin and his temper, his poor sportsmanship, his indifference. Nor could she forget the remark that Mable's mother had made. It rankled her mind like a small sore that kept getting larger. And she knew all this had come because she had not shrugged it off right away. And the girls—what was she going to do with them if they did not improve?

She was tired, but it was a weariness of mind and spirit. She wanted to feel free again, free of the heavy responsibility that was weighing upon her. This task was too great for her. She walked to the window. Several brightly colored leaves came floating down to the ground. Soon autumn would be past, and she had seen so little of it! She had not gathered any nuts nor raked leaves. There were so many things she had not done that she had always done before. Laura gazed at the distant hills. They looked deeply purple in the autumn sunshine. She marveled at their beauty. And looking at them, Laura realized what she needed. She needed the quietness of the trees, the stillness of nature that was so restful to the spirit.

She looked back at her desk. There were papers to check and lessons to prepare. Resolutely she turned and went out the door. Nearby were the woods, and now she followed the path that led to them. The squirrels chattered and scolded above her. Who was this who dared to come and disturb their peace? Their bushy tails jerked and their bright eyes watched the intruder inquisitively. There was the twitter of the birds. In the distance came the mournful call of a dove. The leaves rustled gently. A nut dropped to the ground, and in all this was the deep quiet of the trees.

As Laura looked at them, with their branches lifted out and upwards to the sky, she thought of the poem, "Trees," by Joyce Kilmer, and several lines repeated themselves in her mind.

A tree that looks at God all day,
And lifts her leafy arms to pray.

It was a favorite poem, one she had learned years ago in school. Now as she gazed about, she tried to push all her troubling thoughts out of her mind. She tried to think only of the goodness and greatness of God. And what could be more beautiful than nature? Nothing that was made was ugly. When storms came and uprooted trees or broke a limb, soon soft mosses and vines would grow over the wounds, hiding the scars and healing what had been hurt. All nature was blended together in a way that glorified the Creator.

Laura sat on an old log. The woodsy smell of earth and leaves and trees was invigorating and refreshing.

She was not sure how long she sat there, but gradually a peace filled her. Her school troubles seemed to melt into the background. She thought of Calvin. She had talked to him about governing his spirit. Now she saw she had need of the same advice. Her own spirit became too involved, was too easily frustrated. She needed to keep her spirit calm and quiet, instead of letting problems annoy and eat like a canker on the inside.

The sun was low in the sky. It was time to return, or Aunt Rachel would become worried. Laura knew as she made her way back, that she did not want to stop teaching. She would not lay the burden down if she could. She could not explain quite what she had received in the woods, but she knew that God had given her what she needed to go on.

Chapter 8

Breakthrough

The stove, sitting at the side of the room, had always given Laura the feeling that here was a benign friend. There was something about its squat, round shape, its mute appearance, that seemed benevolent. Now, as Laura prepared to start a good fire, she anticipated the welcome warmth that would issue from its fat sides. Deftly she applied the match, and then she watched eagerly to see the flame lapping over the wood. But the flame flickered weakly and died away. Oh well, she would strike another match. She had always enjoyed starting a fire.

She glanced out the window. She had come early to catch up on what she had not done yesterday. She did not regret the walk she had taken. It must have been the last beautiful day of autumn, for when she had awakened that morning, a cold drizzly rain was coming down. A raw wind was blowing, and the sky was overcast and grey. The grey-blue mountains looked cold and distant.

She looked at the clock. The precious minutes were flying. Quickly she applied another match. This too, made a weak flutter or two and then was gone. She went to the trash can. She would stuff it with paper. There! Finally it burned.

Laura hastened to her desk. But not for long. The friendly stove began to smoke. As she hastened over, it gave a hearty belch, and fine soot and ashes settled gently over her. The wind! That was it, coming from the wrong direction. She turned the damper, and the smoke poured out in profusion. Hastily, she turned it in the opposite direction. And then there was silence. She opened the door and saw that she had smothered the flame.

When the children arrived, Laura was still hard at it. And looking at the shivering, damp children, she decided the stove resembled a black, cold monster. She sighed. She had prayed for guidance that morning. She had prayed for the children. But she had not reckoned on the stove. And she had come to school with such a fresh resolve. *But at least,* she told herself, *I am battling with the stove, not one of the children.* She looked at the front of her dress. And just that morning she had put on a clean one.

But the children considered the whole thing something of a lark. "I'll bring in more wood," Calvin offered. Before she could protest that there was a boxful behind the stove, he was gone. Soon he came in bearing a great armload. The other boys quickly left to do the same.

"That's enough. Oh well, put it down if you have it in here anyway." She looked regretfully at the tracked and muddy floor.

Calvin dashed to the door where three or four more were staggering under mighty loads. "Teacher says it's enough."

"Aw, she wants my load yet."

"This log is just what she needs." Henry puffed majestically. He gave Laura a beseeching look.

"Well, bring it in, boys," Laura said. She could not bear to see them looking so disappointed. The room was in disorder. It needed a good cleaning. How different the trials of a day could turn out. She had come to school, feeling fortified and strong, eager to face the day with the children. No, she had not counted on the stove. Was this God's way of helping her learn patience?

She glanced around the room. The children were jovial. Why not relax and be jolly with them? They did not seem to mind the cold. They chattered and moved about like so many sparrows. Then she saw that Betty,

Mable, and Sally were in a tight little huddle in the back of the room. The rest of the children were milling about happily.

Harvey was patiently helping Marcus take off his boots. George and Calvin were showing each other what stunts they could do. At the present their differences were forgotten. George and Calvin seemed to have a quiet little feud between them. George was a little older, but Calvin was the better ball player, and George was inclined to feel jealous. He would do little things to provoke Calvin, and then Calvin treated George the same way. But neither one would stoop so low as to tattle on the other. In spite of their rivalry, they seemed to have an unwritten law of loyalty between them, and when major differences came up, they sided with each other.

Now, as Laura watched the two boys, she thought of George's parents. They were very concerned about him. He was impulsive and hasty, quick to take offense. But whenever she had problems with him, he was always ready and willing to admit his fault. She knew that she had the full support of his parents, and she felt it was due to home training that George was kept from being one of her problem children.

She noted that Henry's brother Walter was seated at his desk, reading. He was a placid, easygoing little boy, as good-natured as Henry, but inclined to be lazy. If he made an out when they played ball, he would chuckle good-naturedly and retire under the shade tree to watch the rest of the inning.

Laura's glance came back to the girls, and her heart was heavy. Was Mable's mother upset again? It was hard telling. How could she get them to mingle with all the girls? She remembered what Aunt Rachel had advised her to do. And Laura felt a deep thankfulness for her Uncle Romans. She knew she had had too much pride in the beginning to confide in them. When she had really analyzed that feeling of reluctance to talk to them about her troubles, she knew that secretly she had been afraid they would think less of her if they knew what troubles she was having. But it had been the minister's sermon that Sunday that had awakened her. "That sermon, it seemed, had been preached especially for her. "Pride," the minister had said, "can show in the way a person dresses. It can also be hidden away, deep in one's heart. Some people have too much pride to ask for advice or to admit they are wrong, too much pride to say, 'I'm sorry.' " The minister had brought out many things that resulted from pride and had given Laura so much to think about. One can always *feel* anger or discouragement. But pride can come so subtly, so stealthily into one's heart, that one is not aware it is there.

A verse the minister had quoted stood out in her memory. "Every one that is proud in heart is an abomination to the LORD: though hand join in hand, he shall not be unpunished" (Proverbs 16:5).

Laura did not know what made her think of all this now. Perhaps it was the thought of Aunt Rachel. *All teachers,* Laura thought to herself, *should have someone wise they can confide in, someone they can trust to discuss their problems with.*

Aunt Rachel had advised Laura to arrange some supervised activities for the girls. Something that would involve them all. "Especially when cold weather comes," she had said. "When we went to school," Aunt Rachel added, "the teacher taught us to knit and do other handwork. The older ones helped the younger ones, and we loved it. But there are many other possibilities too."

Laura knew that would help. Working together on a project would draw them closer together, especially if the older ones could help the younger ones. There were Clara and Linda in the sixth grade. They chummed with the younger girls, but sometimes when Sally appeared at odds with Betty and Mable, she would be extra friendly to Clara and Linda. Laura knew that was not good. The girls should stay together as a group and all be friends. As for the boys, they made no trouble at all in that respect.

But the girls were different.

She noticed that Sally was beckoning to her. Laura took a deep breath. What now? Had Mable's mother been so upset that she was sending a complaint through Mable? But no, she *must not* jump to conclusions. Nonetheless, Laura steeled herself.

"Yes, girls?" Laura breathed a prayer that she would remain calm and unruffled, wise to know what to do or say.

The girls were visibly nervous. They stood with downcast eyes, and Mable was twisting her hankie in a tight, mouse-like knot.

Betty took a deep breath. "We are sorry for the way we have been acting," she began bravely. She looked with beseeching eyes at Laura.

"We decided we would stay in at recess. We thought it would help us to remember." Mable blinked to keep back her tears.

"We want to try and do better," Sally added.

For a moment there was silence. This was so unexpected, so opposite of what Laura had imagined, that words failed her just then.

She tried to speak. But what could she say? What words could express what their apology meant to her? Finally she managed to say, "Thank you, girls. I appreciate this more than I can say."

Relief and joy spread over the girls' faces. Gone were the evasive looks.

When Laura returned to the room, the stove was still emitting little puffs of smoke whenever the fancy seemed to strike it. The floor was tracked. Calvin, brandishing a great stick of wood, was giving merry chase after the other boys, in, around, and sometimes over the desks. And above all the clamor, everyone seemed to be talking at the top of their voices.

But Laura smiled. The room seemed glorified. Dirt could be cleaned up with soap and water. The tap of the bell would silence the noise. But she was not thinking of that. She knew now with certainty that teaching *was* worth all the heartache, all the tears, all the prayers.

To think that Sally—willful, resentful Sally—had actually taken upon herself a punishment . . . and Betty and Mable . . . willing and ready to confess and do better. There were no words to describe Laura's feelings just then.

Chapter 9

A Key to Calvin

"Calvin, stop making that racket and get busy." Laura was busy with a class at the blackboard, but she knew without turning her head that Calvin was contriving to make some kind of noise.

Calvin tried to scowl, but he had to grin. He put his ruler down on his desk. "I don't got nothing to do."

"You don't have anything to do," Laura corrected him. "Did you do your reading?"

Calvin nodded, but smugly. He looked about the room with a half-bored yet interested look.

Laura sighed. She could imagine how his lesson looked. The rest of the class were still toiling away on reading. Now he would sit there with nothing to do, and he was sure to do something. Why did he always have to work at such breakneck speed? "Write the wise saying that's on the board, for handwriting practice, Calvin." She turned to the class at the board. As soon as she was finished with them, she would look for something to occupy Calvin.

But the third grade was learning borrowing in subtraction. Laura had never known before that there were so many *wrong* ways to subtract! She soon forgot about Calvin.

"See, Karl, you can't take three from two. You have to—" There was a sudden clatter, and Laura, her chalk raised in midair, turned to survey the room. "Calvin, please keep your books in your desk, not on top. No wonder you drop them." She turned back to the class. *That look in Calvin's eyes . . . was that really all he had done?* The look on his face and the suppressed giggles of the children made Laura wonder. But sometimes it was easier to take for granted she knew what happened and leave it at that.

The class at the board had been contenting themselves by drawing little figures and faces. The problems were all worked wrong except one. Laura sighed audibly. She had explained it all so clearly. She tried to gather her patience together. "Now then," she began. She tried to sound brisk and enthusiastic. "You must keep your mind on what you are doing. We'll start all over."

Small hands gripped the chalk. Karl's face drew into a frown as he tried to follow each step of the directions. Because he had a new piece of chalk, he tried to write with only two fingers. It was so much easier to write with a whole piece! He gave the number two an extra flourish, and accidently the chalk slipped out of his fingers. With a little crash, it dropped to the floor, breaking into three or four pieces. He gazed sadly down.

"Pick it up, Karl," Laura said, shortly. She bit her lip. The others, glad for a little diversion, turned and watched attentively as he picked up the pieces. "Well, go on with your problems. I'm sure Karl can pick it up without you watching." Laura stopped, sorry she had spoken so sharply. Just now words had a way of coming out before she could think.

Rufus turned back to his problem with a sigh. Then with sudden inspiration, he set to work. He added his first column, carrying a ten, and subtracting the next column.

"Oh, Rufus," it was Laura's voice behind him, and it did not sound happy at all. "You don't carry when you subtract. Erase—"

There was a slight commotion, and Laura glanced around and saw Calvin was wearing a paper mask on his face. The small children were gazing at him in fascination. Just then Calvin turned and glanced at Laura to see if all was safe.

"Calvin, bring me that thing!" There was a heavy silence as he brought the mask up to

Laura's desk. He looked sheepish.

"When did you make this?"

"Aw, just a few minutes ago." He shifted his weight from one foot to the other.

"You know better, Calvin, making a disturbance like that. Did you do that handwriting?"

"Yes, Teacher." He stood looking meekly down. *Like some innocent lamb,* Laura thought, *acting as if he doesn't know better.* She looked down at the mask. Calvin had indeed looked so comical that if she had not been so mortified, she would have had to laugh.

She suddenly remembered the conversation with Uncle Roman the evening before. He had said he hoped she would want to teach again next term. "The second year should be a lot easier," he had said. Laura had agreed. Perhaps she would teach again. There was something about it that drew her. It was certainly not the easiest job. No, there was a hardness about it that made it so challenging. It took your all. And even that was not enough—it took a complete dependence on God.

But teaching here at this same school? That was something else. She knew, though she would not admit it to anyone, there was one drawback. She did not know how she was going to get through even one term with Calvin, let alone another! She was not the right teacher for Calvin, and it seemed a mistake that he was her pupil. He was unpredictable. When she was feeling angry, he could make her laugh. And she did not want to get angry. She wanted to be quiet and calm. No matter what happened, she wanted to stay serene, to rise above those feelings of frustration and annoyance. Nor did she want to laugh at his antics. How could she help Calvin, feeling as she did? No, Calvin needed an experienced, wise teacher. And she knew deep down that he was like a stumbling block in her path.

Laura gazed at the mask lying crisply on her desk. The third graders were restless and bored. How were they to learn with so many interruptions? And she was feeling cross and impatient with them.

"Calvin." She tried not to sound as cross as she felt. "Put the mask in the trash can."

What now? She would talk with him at recess, but until then. . . . "Take your geography book and go out to the entry and study it there. For the rest of the period you will stay out there."

If only I could talk with his parents! Laura had met them, but there had been little chance to talk. Surely that would help, talking over Calvin's behavior with them. Or would it? She thought of Mable's mother. Parents were not always how you expected them to be.

Laura glanced at the clock. It was time for the first grade phonics lesson, and she was not finished with the class at the board. "Go to your seats," she told them. They needed to do something else anyway. Drilling too long on the same lesson was tiring. They could have another session at the board later.

At recess, Laura took time to talk with Calvin again. "Do you realize what you are doing, Calvin, when you disturb the class? You are hindering them from doing their work. You are hurting all of us, not just yourself." Calvin stared at the wall. And Laura looked at him dejectedly. She was gaining nothing with him at all. She searched her own heart. Had she dealt wisely with him that morning? She had known he had his work done. She had given him almost nothing but commands and do nots. She should get something lined up, something for him to do when he was finished, something worthwhile, so he wouldn't be idling those minutes away. *But why*, she wondered a little resentfully, *must I spend so much more time and effort with him.*

Calvin was still staring at the wall. *How far apart we are*, she thought hopelessly. "Calvin," she spoke slowly. She knew he was expecting a punishment, and she knew also that he was fairly bursting with eagerness to go out and play ball. "I'm going to let you go on out and play. Next time there will be a punishment."

Calvin looked almost startled. Without a word, however, he turned and hurried out.

She heard happy shouts from the playground. Of course, Calvin's side was cheering because Calvin was coming. If only he were not such a good player! Calvin played hard and fast. He put all his effort, all his might, into the game, and Calvin played to win! He needed his recess to run off his energy. *But that's another thing. He is a good player, but a poor loser.* Laura sighed. There were so many things that needed to be worked on. And right now she needed to be out on the playground too.

She paused at her desk. Such a jumble of papers! *What is this?* She picked it up and studied it thoughtfully. Ah, yes, the handwriting she had given Calvin to do. For some reason it brought a lump into her throat. She had expected him to write it two or three times. Instead, Calvin had written on both sides of the paper. The whole sides were covered, and even the margins had been filled up with Calvin's scrawly writing.

Why had he written so much? As Laura stared at the paper, she felt as though a key were turning. *Calvin wants to have something to do . . . or . . . is he trying to please me?* Either way, it was a beginning.

Chapter 10

Trouble at the Tree House

"I have a headache and a stomachache and a sore throat." Rufus smiled his sweet little smile and looked at his teacher to see if she was fully grasping what he was saying.

She wasn't. It was time for the bell, and Laura was frantically trying to check a late paper. All she heard was "ache and ache." Rufus talked in a quiet voice, and Laura usually had to strain her ears to get the full benefit of his words. But now she did not murmur an absentminded "um, hum" the way she sometimes did when she did not catch something clearly. She stopped her work in midair and looked at Rufus's face.

Laura secretly considered Rufus her pathetic pupil. For one thing he was so sweet. He was too meek and timid and quiet to do anything he shouldn't, and yet she sometimes felt impatient with him. Then with sorrow and remorse she would look at his thin, small features. His fault was to gaze absorbedly at the other children and meanwhile forget his own work.

"Get busy, Rufus," she would remind him. For a while his little head would be bent over his work. Then he would see Henry go for a dictionary or hear Susie ask a question, and Rufus would forget again that he had anything to do except watch the other children. He was slow in catching on to things. While she explained to his class, he would be gazing dreamily at the other children. Invariably, she would have to explain the whole lesson over to him later.

Now, when Rufus spoke of aches, Laura wondered. She wanted the children to come to school if at all possible, but she did not want them to come if they were sick. Why was he in school if he ached all over? "Rufus, how long have you been sick?" she demanded. Then she realized she was pointing her pencil at him as if he had committed some crime.

Rufus smiled his patient little smile. "Oh, I'm not sick now."

"But what did you say was wrong with you?"

"Oh, I said I have had stomachache and headache and sore throat."

"Then you feel all right now?"

Rufus smiled again. A longsuffering smile,

as though giving allowance for his teacher.

"Yes, I feel all right now. This was last week I had stomachache and headache and sore throat."

"Then it didn't last long?" Laura was still rather baffled.

Rufus looked at her trustingly, as if certain she understood now. "No. You see, it was this way. I was hiding in the barn, and there was some fertilizer in there, and it made me a headache, and when I coughed, it went into my stomach and made my throat sore."

When did all this happen? Laura wondered. Aloud she said, "You weren't tasting it, were you, Rufus?"

"No, I was just hiding in the barn." Rufus smiled.

"Well, I am glad you are all right now."

Rufus nodded contentedly. He went to his desk with a satisfied look.

Larua hurried to ring the bell. *Next time I am impatient with Rufus,* she thought, *I hope I can remember how patient he is with me.*

But her musings were stopped short as Christopher came panting up to her desk.

"What did you want Christopher? And don't cry," for she saw that he was in tears. "Crying won't help anyway."

"The boys don't, don't—" blubbered Chriss, "don't let us help on the tree house."

"What boys?" Laura demanded.

"Why, Henry and George and them."

Leaving the bell on the desk, she followed him outside. The girls and those boys who did not care to work on the tree house were playing tag together. All but Mable. She had followed her little brother inside and was watching to see what would happen.

All through the golden days of autumn the children had played ball with dedicated zeal. Then one day someone announced that he was tired of playing ball. And surprisingly enough, everyone was tired of it. When Laura had asked what they wanted to play, they had shrugged their shoulders and looked at each other.

"Let's build a tree house," one suggested.

"We did last year," chimed in another, seeing Laura's doubtful expression.

And so, after due instructions, the boys had fallen to work with mighty fervor. They came to school armed with broken tools salvaged from home shops and junk. There were pieces of wire, tin, and boards. Rufus brought a broken piece of pipe "to talk through," he explained.

Laura realized now she had been overconfident. They had gotten along so well together the first days that she had not bothered to check on them to see how they really were getting along. But, of course, Chriss was so easily upset. . . .

They were met by Calvin and George,

who wore hurt, aggrieved expressions.

"Henry and Karl and them don't let us work with them."

"And Henry threw a log at Calvin." Calvin nodded at George's words to verify this shocking bit of news.

"A log? Surely not! Why, I don't think Henry could lift one, much less throw one." Whatever had come over the boys? Something was drastically wrong. Usually it was Calvin and George who were at odds with each other. Even so, they were not the kind to tattle. Henry and Karl were mild-tempered and easy to get along with.

"Now, boys, tell me what is wrong here," Laura said when she had them assembled in the room.

The boys glared at each other. Finally Henry spoke, and it did not sound like good-natured Henry at all. "We wanted to work by ourselves for a change."

"All Calvin does is mess up the whole works," Karl added.

"Just how do you mean?" Laura asked sternly.

"Aw, he won't make it right," Matthew said grimly.

"And George hides the nails, and Chriss gets in the way."

"And we wanted to make it right, a real tree house." Henry's freckles stood out aggrievedly.

The opposite side spoke up. "Henry thinks he's the boss."

"And he threw a log," added another.

"Boys, a log is too big to throw."

"But it was," George insisted. "He threw it hard, too."

"How big was it?" Laura knew that in a skirmish, Calvin would surely outdo Henry. He was a head taller than Henry and was quick and nimble, whereas Henry was stocky and slow-motioned. Calvin and George were good at many things, but they were clumsy with a saw and hammer. Was that the problem? One side wanted to make it right, and George and Calvin had probably tired of the work but wanted to be included.

"The log was about the size of, well, it was larger than that there." George pointed to the spokes of a chair.

"Now boys, that would be a stick, not a log. You were exaggerating, George, and that is not being honest." Laura looked severely at George.

"But it was round, so I thought it was a log." George looked at Calvin, who still maintained an injured silence.

"Well, I think you are all at fault. Why don't you apologize and see how nice you can get along together." Laura looked hopefully from one boy to another. But the boys remained stony-faced.

"It is not kind to mess things up," she said,

looking at Calvin, "or to hide the nails. And no one likes to be bossed around either. And I don't want any of you throwing sticks. Can't you see how each one has failed?" She looked from one gloomy face to the other.

There was no sign of repentance on any of the faces. Instead, they began to voice their grievances again.

"I just won't work down there if Chriss tags along," said one.

Another complained, "Henry won't let me even use his hammer anymore."

Laura walked to the window and looked out. She felt completely at a loss. *My good boys . . . except Calvin, of course . . . acting like this? How can I make them feel sorry? How can I make each one see his own faults?*

The boys stood waiting. She knew she must do something, and she felt empty. *Please God, what shall I do?* A Bible verse came to her mind. "All Scripture is given by inspiration of God, and is profitable for doctrine, for reproof, for correction. . . ." That was it, the Bible! It would have the answer. She turned from the window. "Come, boys, we want to look up some verses that tell us how we should treat each other.

Reluctantly, the boys found seats. There was a strained silence. "Karl, you may get the Bibles and pass them out." Looking at the boys, Laura thought of their parents. All

96

of them, excepting Calvin's parents, had come and talked to her about their children. All of them had shown great concern and interest.

She took a Bible. "Can any of you think of some verses that would apply to our problem?" There was still profound silence. "Well, let's find the Golden Rule first. Does anyone know where it is? Yes, that's right," she nodded to George. "It's in Matthew. Why don't we read the Beatitudes first," she said impulsively.

They took turns, each reading a verse. As they read, Laura's mind wandered. She should have picked out verses about being kind and esteeming others better than themselves. They had come to the ninth verse. "Blessed are the peacemakers: for they shall be called the children of God." "None of you were practicing that, were you?" she asked as she looked up from the Bible. She was touched to see how moved they looked. George, who was sitting opposite from her was blinking hard to keep back the tears. "Let's find Matthew 7:12." Laura looked down at her Bible. She had a strong desire to weep. She realized that while her mind had been searching for other verses, the boys had been taking to heart the verses they had been reading.

Laura could not put in words what she felt just then. Around the family altar, these boys had knelt and prayed with their parents that morning. They had been taught from earliest childhood that the Scriptures were the sacred words of God. Now, as she saw how moved they were, it seemed to her that it must be the prayers of those parents who cared so deeply for their children. Slowly she read the Golden Rule. "Therefore all things whatsoever ye would that men should do to you, do ye even so to them: for this is the law and the prophets." She saw there was no need to read or search for more.

She marveled to see how changed the boys were, so humble and subdued. Gone were the accusing looks and stony faces. She struggled to keep back the tears as they made peace among themselves.

At the next recess, the boys trooped out happily together, their differences forgotten. As Laura watched them go, she knew they were not the only ones who had learned a lesson that morning.

Chapter 11

Jealousy

"Teacher, something happened just now."

"What happened, Rufus?" Laura turned from the blackboard and glanced at the clock. It was almost time to take up school. If she hurried, she would be able to write the geography questions yet.

"Teacher." Rufus was smiling his patient little smile. "Karl broke the jar where his cocoon was in, and I can't get in to the broom closet for the dustpan."

"Well, did Karl sweep up the glass?"

"He started to, but he stepped in some glass, and now it's bleeding all over," Rufus smiled sweetly.

Bleeding all over? Anxiously, Laura hurried out to the front steps. She saw to her relief that the cut itself was not bad, but Karl had managed to get drops of blood on the steps. "Can you, Dora, please bring me the

Band-aids and the disinfectant in my drawer?"

It was nice in more ways than one, having children right at one's elbow. "Thank you, Dora. You were so quick." She smiled at her dark-eyed little student. "Now be careful, Karl. It has stopped bleeding, so the Band-aid should stay on."

Karl smiled. "Thank you for fixing it." He hobbled cheerfully to his desk, followed by Rufus who would now be his devoted little slave for the rest of the day.

Laura rose from the steps and picked up the dustpan. She would put the broken glass in a box and discard it later. When she opened the broom closet, she was startled to see a figure huddled on one of the boxes. "Why, why, Mable," she gasped. "Whatever are you doing in here? Are you sick?"

She could see at a glance that Mable had been crying. She was twisting a hankie around and around her fingers. At the sight of Laura, the tears started again.

"Can't you tell me what is wrong?" Many things flashed through Laura's mind as she stood there waiting.

Mable shook her head and dabbed at her eyes.

"I'm sorry, Mable. I can't help you if you don't tell me what is wrong." Then a sudden through struck her. "Do Sally and Betty have something to do with this?"

This time there was a silent nod and a long, tearful sigh.

"Won't you tell me what the trouble is?"

"Sally will call me a tattler if I say anything." The tears started again.

"Very well. I'll talk to Sally and Betty." Why hadn't she noticed that something was wrong? How had it been yesterday? She tried to remember. They had played together. And now she remembered that after the bell rang, Betty and Sally had walked in together. But she had thought nothing of it. How was a teacher to know when problems were shaping up? Now it was time for the bell. But another look at Mable's miserable face helped her decide.

She would talk with Betty first. Betty was dependable and could be trusted.

"Betty, Mable is very unhappy. Do you have any idea what is wrong?"

Betty hesitated. Her eyes were troubled as she looked at Laura. "I don't want to get in trouble with Sally or Mable. But, but. . . ."

"You won't be in trouble, Betty. Please go on. I had no idea there was a problem among you girls."

"It's just been this last week or so," Betty said quietly. "Sally says things about Mable, and Mable says things about Sally."

"But sometimes Sally and Mable are together. I don't understand."

"I know. But Mable found out the things

Sally was saying about her behind her back."

"How did Mable find out?"

"Sally told Calvin and Calvin told Chriss, Mable's brother. But Mable didn't start talking about Sally until she found out that Sally was talking about her. And this morning Chriss said something that Calvin said that Sally had told him yesterday, and it upset Mable."

Laura looked at the clock. The minutes marched relentlessly on. "Betty, I want to talk with you girls at recess, but please do not mention this to anyone."

"I won't." Betty walked to her desk, and there was a rather relieved look on her face.

Laura went to the window. The hills were a deep purple-blue. The sun, shining through clouds, enhanced their beauty, causing deep shadows and light that touched them softly. Laura knew she must ring the bell. She longed to go away to some quiet place to think and pray. She rang the bell. But all through the morning, she found it almost impossible to keep her mind on the lessons. She noted with relief when it was time for the morning recess, but the feeling was instantly replaced with a feeling of dread. And in the back of her mind was the thought of Mable's mother and Sally's as well. Inside she shrank from upsetting them again. She wanted them to like her. But she knew she must do what she felt was right.

She remembered a thought from a devotional book. "Whenever we are very concerned for ourselves about other people's opinion, we may be sure we are thinking too little of God and what will please Him."

But what could she say to impress the girls how wrong it is to talk unkindly about each other?

She dismissed the children for recess. "Sally, I want you to stay in . . . and please close the door."

Laura's heart beat fast. She tried to steady herself. "Girls," she began. Sally was gazing out the window, Betty looked troubled and sorry. Mable was again on the verge of tears. "It's not right, is it," she continued, "to talk about each other? I want to read some verses from Proverbs 6. 'These six things doth the LORD hate: yea, seven are an abomination unto him: A proud look, a lying tongue, and hands that shed innocent blood, an heart that deviseth wicked imaginations, feet that be swift in running to mischief, a false witness that speaketh lies, and he that soweth discord among brethren.' " The room was very quiet. But Laura felt a certain strength within her now. She looked at Sally, and her heart ached.

"It's terrible to do something that God hates, and aren't we sowing discord among brethren, or giving a false witness when we talk about each other?"

103

After a slight pause, she continued, "Often it is jealousy that prompts us to speak about others unkindly. We read in the Bible that Satan wanted to have the highest place of honor in heaven. We also read that he is an accuser, and we know what happened to him. What do we gain anyway, by running down another person? Aren't we actually hurting ourselves?"

Laura looked up at the girls. Mable was twisting her hankie. "I'm sorry," she turned to Sally. "I said some things I shouldn't have."

Laura could never put in words the feeling that went through her when a student was willing to confess a fault. All the heartache and headache of teaching faded at such times.

She looked at Sally and she could see that Sally did not want to admit her fault. "I'm sorry," Betty was saying quietly. "Maybe I said some things too I shouldn't have."

Reluctantly, Sally spoke, "I don't think I said so much." She would not look at Laura or the other girls. She had a defensive look on her face as though she thought Laura was making too big an issue of this. Sally bit her lip. Laura, Betty, and Mable waited. "I'm sorry," Sally said, finally.

"Betty, you and Mable may go. Sally," Laura continued after the girls had left, "I think you should have a punishment." But what punishment should she give an eighth grade girl? Stay in at recess? But what would she do? She should do something meaningful.

She looked at Sally and her heart ached. There was a half-defiant, half-repentant look on her face. "Sally," she said, impulsively. "Do you know why I am giving you this punishment?"

Sally looked up and saw the tears in Laura's eyes. She bit her lip and looked away.

"I love you, Sally."

The pride, self-will, and self-defense in Sally's face wilted, and she began to sob quietly.

Laura paused a bit and then went on, "I want you to talk to Calvin. And then I want you to stay in and write a composition on this."

"What do you mean?" Sally looked up.

"I want you to write on the evils of gossip—why it is wrong, what it does, and what the motives are that prompt people to gossip. Use Bible verses and a concordance if you need to. You will work on it at recess."

Sally nodded. "When do you want me to talk to Calvin?"

"Right now, Sally. I'll get him in." She was glad Sally made no objection. And she was very glad to find that Sally seemed sincere in her apology to Calvin. Calvin in turn apologized to Chriss.

On Friday, when Sally handed in her composition, Laura rejoiced. It was well-written, and at the bottom Sally had written two golden words: "I'm sorry."

Chapter 12

Paper Wad

"Magellan gave the name *Pacific* to the calm waters spread before him." Harvey paused and Laura nodded encouragingly.

"That's right, Harvey."

"Then they sailed for three months and twenty days without seeing any land at all."

"And some of the crew died of hunger," said Mable.

"Some of the men even ate the leather that they stripped from the yardarms. They soaked it in the sea." Betty shuddered as she added this bit to the lesson.

Laura always enjoyed the history lessons. The class seemed to like them too. Harvey especially, excelled in history. Now Laura gazed with unseeing eyes out the window. She tried to picture how Magellan had felt, standing on the ship and sighting the blue waters of the mighty ocean . . . then the long days of sailing with no land in sight . . . and the crew sick and dying.

But she was suddenly brought back to reality as a wad of paper went whizzing by.

Startled she gazed after it. She was no longer on a rocking ship with Magellan, looking at the calm waters of the Pacific.

"Who threw that?" she demanded, looking about the room for the culprit and feeling very annoyed.

No one spoke, but most of the children were looking at Calvin. And Calvin, Laura noticed much to her vexation, was trying hard not to laugh.

"Don't speak when you are angry." The words rang in her mind, and Laura swallowed. Those words had sounded easy enough when she had first heard them. But she knew the actual doing was something else. She wanted to take Calvin and shake him—hard. She looked down as she tried to control her voice and her feelings.

"Go out," she said in an ominously quiet voice, "to the broom closet." The room became breathlessly quiet. All rustling of papers and books ceased. The children stared silently as Calvin rose and, trying to look unconcerned, walked out of the room. But Calvin was no longer smiling. After a few more words, she sent the class back to their desks. She could not keep her mind on the lesson now, and everyone else too was conscious of Calvin out in the closet. Everyone knew that Calvin had something coming.

There was no need to tell the children to be quiet. As Laura left the room, she could have heard a pin drop. Outside the door she stopped. If this had been Calvin's first offense for the day, she might not have felt so disgusted. But that morning she had sent him in from the playground. Calvin's team for once (and Laura had been secretly glad of it) was losing the ball game. Calvin had muttered darkly to his team that the sides were unfair. Instantly those words had put Laura on her mettle.

"Those sides *are* fair," Laura had said. Either he would be quiet and play nicely or he could go in to his desk. She had gone in herself then, for it was almost time for the bell, and she wanted to check some problems Rufus was working.

Rufus was indeed having trouble, and Laura was glad she had come in. "Here, Rufus, you forgot to add this." Laura walked to the window and looked out. She could see that Calvin was playing with furious determination. In a moment, she turned back. "That is right, Rufus, you may go now." She followed him out and was just in time to hear the heated argument.

"It's an out. I know it is. Henry didn't touch the base." Calvin's eyes blazed.

"My foot was on base, just as it is now."

Henry's freckles stood out indignantly. The smaller players were accused sometimes of being careless, but Henry was careful. He might be slow, but he knew how to play ball.

"Their side cheats. They—"

"Calvin," said Laura sternly, "go in to your desk."

When Laura came in, Calvin was sulking in his seat. His face resembled a thundercloud. "As big as you are," Laura began, her voice strong with feeling, "you should be ashamed of yourself. Being a good sport is much more important than winning a game." As she looked at his downcast face, which was still dark with feeling, a feeling of pity came over her. Poor Calvin—he had so much growing up to do. Her voice was sad and stern as she told him he was acting worse than the first graders. His ability to play a game well meant nothing if he could not accept a defeat without losing his temper.

Calvin had said nothing. He had stared moodily into space.

And now—this!

Laura took a deep breath. She was too easy with Calvin. And the very idea that he looked on the whole thing as a joke filled her with mortification.

Calvin looked up from the box he was sitting on when she entered. She noted with secret satisfaction that he did look a little worried.

"Why were you throwing paper around, Calvin?"

"Aw, I just meant to throw it into the trash can."

"But you know better than that. You disturbed the whole room." Laura looked hard at Calvin.

"I was just trying it for once."

"And why weren't you doing your science lesson?"

"I'm all finished."

"You have your work all done?"

He nodded and sighed.

Then Laura remembered. She recalled Calvin's handwriting paper, filled up to overflowing with writing. She had resolved she would give him worthwhile things to do. But she had forgotten. Even so, Calvin's behavior had somewhat improved in the classroom.

But now she was feeling too annoyed with him to praise him for the efforts he had put forth in writing that day. She looked at him moodily. Of all her students, Calvin tried her the most.

He seemed to bring out all her worst feelings—anger, mortification, annoyance. And she knew unless she could rise above these feelings, she could never be victor. Always they left her feeling deeply ashamed and humbled. She could not help Calvin feeling as she did. Calvin desperately

111

needed a good teacher.

But now Calvin needed a punishment. She knew how much he loved recess. He would have to stay in.

Calvin nodded. She noticed suddenly to her annoyance that he was trying not to smile. He turned his head away. He tried to look sober but he could not.

"You can just tell me what is so funny, Calvin." Inwardly Laura was feeling more vexed than ever. Giving him a punishment, then having him laugh about it!

Calvin looked helplessly at his teacher.

"I'm waiting, Calvin."

He tried to look sober, and there was silent appeal in his dark eyes. "You won't like it if I tell you."

"Go on and tell me, Calvin." Surely she could not feel more irked than she was feeling now.

Still he hesitated, but he saw there was no getting around it.

"I just happened to think how you looked when that wad of paper whizzed past your head."

"Oh, so I looked funny?" That helpless feeling was sweeping over her again.

Calvin nodded. He tried to look sober but he failed altogether. "You looked mighty surprised."

"Well, Calvin, do not let it happen again," Laura said quietly.

When Calvin returned to the classroom, everyone was still breathlessly quiet and working with silent fervor. They gave Calvin a searching look and returned to their tasks at hand.

The afternoon passed quietly. An episode in the broom closet always brought on the children's best behavior. Although it was anybody's guess just what had taken place inside, no one cared to run the risk of finding out!

As Laura dismissed for the last recess, Rufus came up to her desk. "Teacher, I can't find my boots."

"Where did you leave them, Rufus?"

"I wore them down to the tree house last week, but I can't remember if I brought them back or not." Rufus smiled a distressed little smile.

"We'll go look for them right now, Rufus." She took his little hand, and they set out.

Laura was glad for a little walk in the woods. Not until she was down at the tree house did she remember that she had forgotten to keep Calvin in. *Of course he went out to play with the rest,* she thought. *Well, he will have to take his punishment tomorrow.*

They found the boots, and Rufus's face lighted up with relief. "I'm glad a bear didn't get them."

"So am I, but there aren't any bears around here, Rufus."

"Well then, a panther."

"But there are no panthers around either."

"Well, what could have gotten them, Teacher?"

"Umm . . . I suppose a dog could have carried them off."

"Then I'm glad a dog didn't carry them off."

"I'm glad too, Rufus." They smiled at each other companionably.

When they got back to the schoolhouse, the children were playing happily. Laura went in to check the time. She glanced at the clock and then at her desk. A piece of paper was lying on top which caught her eye. She read at a glance, "I must not throw paper wads. I must not throw stuff. I must not throw books. I must not throw pencils. I must not throw trash." The list went on and on. It was unmistakably Calvin's writing with Calvin's name written boldly at the top.

Laura took a deep breath and sat down. She had told him to stay in at recess, but she had not said how long. And he had written something on his own accord.

She remembered how cross she had been with him that day. He had been honest. He had risked her displeasure when he told her what he was laughing about, and he had not wanted to tell. She had seen that. She knew what it was like having to laugh when you least wanted too. And when she had forgotten, Calvin had remembered.

She walked to the window and looked out. The mountains seemed to hold wisdom and strength for her. And now as she saw their beauty and magnificence, she felt small and undone. Calvin had not seen how cross she had been on the inside, but God had.

The clock ticked away in the empty room. Laura knew what she must do. She went to the door, and seeing Karl nearby, she told him to tell Calvin to come in.

A little later Calvin made his appearance. He looked wary, on his guard.

"Calvin," began Laura, "I forgot to remind you to stay in and write something. But I see you did anyway. You did write this at recess?"

Calvin nodded. "I wrote as fast as I could. Then I went out."

"I want to thank you for obeying me, though I had forgotten." She drew a sheet of paper out of her desk. "I also want to tell you how pleased I was when I found this writing on my desk that day." Together they looked at the handwriting that covered the paper. And the words seemed to stare up at them, "Falsehood is cowardice; truth is courage."

"I hope you can remember that always, Calvin. And, Calvin," Laura went on, "I'm sorry I was so cross with you today. You did not behave, but neither should I have been

115

so cross."

Calvin looked up at his teacher and then down at the writing on the paper. "Falsehood is cowardice; truth is courage," he read again, silently. "I'm sorry," his voice was scarcely above a whisper, "I'm sorry I did not behave today."

And when Laura looked up, he had gone.

Chapter 13

Calvin Wins the Ball Game

"Don't cry, Christopher. See, it's hardly more than a scratch."

But Chriss, taking a fresh look at the scratched knee, only cried harder.

"It's worse 'n I thought. It's bleeding awful bad."

Laura dabbed at the knee with a bit of clean cloth. She was trying hard not to feel disgusted. Nor did it help matters any to have Mable hovering at her elbow, dripping with sympathy for Chriss.

"Mom says the boys are just too rough."

Laura did not want to have another encounter with Mable and Chriss's mother, but she felt she could not let this pass. "All that the boys are doing is playing ball." She tried to speak calmly and quietly, but she felt annoyed. "It's no one's fault that Christopher fell."

"But they were after him to get him out, and Calvin chased him so hard."

"Was Calvin trying to tag you with the ball, Chriss?"

Christopher shook his head. "It was Henry."

Laura was relieved. Christopher and Calvin did not get along as well as she wished. Calvin might easily have given Chriss an extra push.

"What made you think it was Calvin?" she asked, turning to Mable.

"I heard Calvin say to get him out, and I thought I saw him running."

"Always be sure before your accuse someone of something. Besides, even if Calvin had tried to get Chriss out, that's no telling he would have pushed him down on purpose."

The knee had stopped bleeding and Laura put antiseptic on the scratch, and then a bandage. Christopher's tears turned to smiles as he saw the bandage.

The poor boy can't help it he is babied and over-protected all the time, Laura thought. She wished she could feel more warmth and love for him. "Now I'm going out to play. You come along, Chriss," she told him.

The children were playing ball with renewed zeal. The first snow had not lasted long, and though it was a cold day, the sun shone brightly.

The sides were evenly matched. They had agreed that the side batting would back catch for the opposite side and try to get any players out who ran for home plate. There was always a great show made of trying to catch the ball as it came flying in when a runner dashed for home. Several narrow escapes were made.

Then Calvin's side came in to bat, and the opposite side was two runs ahead. When Calvin batted, he made a home run, and there were wild cheers and yells. Laura, who was playing on third base, watched as George came up to bat.

On a day like this, George and Calvin were the best of friends. They were both on the same side, and George had no pangs of jealousy. The two boys cheered each other on as each took his turn to bat.

Calvin had taken the catcher's mitt and he had his normal determined-to-win look in his eyes. "Don't make an out. You just can't make an out," he was telling George. "We've already got two."

On the first pitch, George made a mighty swing, and the ball flew out into the field. There was a breathless moment when everyone thought Henry would catch the ball. But he missed. Then there was wild cheering as George sped around the bases. He came to third. He hesitated.

"Come on, come on, you can make it.

YOU CAN MAKE IT. COME ON. No, stay there, STAY THERE. STAY THERE!" But George was streaking for home.

"Home it. Home it!" they yelled for the ball. Calvin was jumping up and down. Harvey, with his steady aim, sent the ball flying home into Calvin's hands just as George went sliding into home. For an instant, Calvin seemed to hesitate. Then he tagged George as he touched home, or was it an instant before? For a moment, there was a speechless, breathless silence.

Then, "That was no out!"

"No, it was a tie. Tie goes to the runner, doesn't it, Teacher?"

Laura was silent. It had been so close she was not sure herself. She looked at Calvin. He stood red-faced, the ball still in his hand. They had worked so hard for that run. "What was it, Calvin?" she asked then. She wondered what he would say.

Calvin was silent. That was most unusual for such a crucial part of the game. Calvin was always so sure of himself. He swallowed. "It was an out. Come on. That's three outs." He marched out to the field.

Calvin's side was taken back. They had been sure Calvin would call it a tie. They were too stunned to protest. The opposite side came in quietly, without the usual shouts of victory. Calvin calling it an out when he could have called it a tie? This was so unexpected, so unlike Calvin, they were speechless. But everyone knew Calvin had done the right thing.

Even George was silent and thoughtful as he went out to the ball field. He wanted to win as badly as anyone, and that one run would have put them ahead. George kicked second base thoughtfully as he watched the opposite side get lined up to bat. He glanced over at Calvin who was playing between second and third.

Calvin was glancing his way too. "Say, George, why don't you take my place here, and I'll be outfielder. Harvey is first to bat and he usually knocks 'em way out."

George nodded agreement. "Suits me. You can catch his flies better than I can anyway."

"Aw, I've got a better mitt," Calvin said modestly.

The tone of the game changed. The side that came in tried to play fair too.

Feeling a sudden need to be alone, Laura returned to the schoolhouse. Her heart seemed to swell within her. Calvin could have called it a tie. It had been that close. But he had played fair. She remembered all the times she had talked to him about being a good sport, about playing for the enjoyment of it, about practicing the Golden Rule.

She knew she did not deserve the wonderfully happy feeling that filled her now. How many times she had despaired and had been provoked and annoyed with Calvin! She could not see with her eyes all Calvin's inner struggles. She had no way of knowing how hard he really tried or how greatly he struggled to do the right things. She thought of the other boys. Henry for instance—easygoing, good-natured Henry had his faults too, but they did not stand out sharply like Calvin's. And in a boy like Calvin, she saw faults and failures and forgot the good that was also there.

After the bell had rung and the children were in their seats again, Laura spoke to Calvin before the whole room. "I want to thank you, Calvin, for playing a good game. We all know how hard you try to win, but you won more than a game today. I know it isn't easy to tag someone out on your side. But that is what you did, and you called it an out." Laura wished she could show Calvin how happy he had made her and how thankful she was.

Calvin tried to look sober, but he looked up and seeing the other children smiling, he had to smile too, a happy, boyish grin.

"The game goes much better when everyone practices the Golden Rule, doesn't it?"

That weekend, Laura went for the groceries for Uncle Romans. Pushing the cart before her, she saw Mable and Christopher's mother coming around the aisle, and her heart gave a great thump. For the instant the little woman saw her, she came bearing down upon her with great speed. Laura tried to smile, but her thoughts were running wildly. *What now? She is probably upset because of the way I talked to Mable, or Chriss . . . I didn't baby them. . . .*

"Hello, Laura, I certainly am glad to see you. Why, I was wanting to talk to you just as soon as I had a chance."

"Oh." Laura swallowed. "Well, I just happened to come in for the groceries and—"

"I was so beat out when Christopher came home that day and had his knee all bandaged up. He—"

"Yes," Laura interrupted, "they were playing ball, and of course they have their tumbles—"

"Yes, Mable told me they were playing ball. But I don't know. Christopher is so little yet. But I wanted to tell you how glad I was that you put antiseptic on it and wrapped it up. He is so susceptible to infections. Seems like one can't be careful enough."

"Well, I—"

"Excuse me, but are you ready to go now?" Mable's father was tapping his wife on the shoulder. Apologetically he added to Laura, "We came in with the neighbors, and they are ready to go home. I hate to make them wait." He was a good-natured, kindly looking man.

"Yes, yes, I'm ready, and thanks again, Laura. You tell us if you have any trouble," she said over her shoulder as she hurried away.

Laura watched them leave. She felt slightly breathless. *How different things can turn out from what a person expects!* She shook her head. *The little woman is appreciative!* And a verse she had learned years ago came to her mind:

There's not so much good in the best of us
And not so much bad in the worst of us
That it behooves any of us
To talk about the rest of us.

Chapter 14

Pneumonia

Henry had important news that morning. Laura could tell, just by the way he walked. He was walking briskly for Henry, and as he saw other children approaching in the opposite direction, he ran the length of the schoolyard. He puffed as he came into the schoolhouse.

"Good morning, Henry," Laura said pleasantly. She tried to look more sober than she felt, for she felt a strong inclination to laugh.

"Did you hear about Karl?" He came up to her desk and stood before her, his face gravely excited.

Just the way he said it, struck a little feeling of fear into her heart. But then, she knew Henry better by now.

"No, I didn't, Henry. Did something happen?" She could not help but feel a little anxious.

Henry shook his head somberly. "You know what?" He came closer, so that he could see just how she took this news. His freckles stood out in sober excitement. "He's in the hospital!" He paused and took a deep breath, waiting to see what Laura would do.

"In the hospital? But why?"

Henry took another deep breath. He looked around. Other children were hastening to Laura's desk, and he must hurry or someone else would beat him to it. "He's got pneumonia."

"Oh, he must be sick." The thought of Karl—small and thin for his age—with pneumonia was rather alarming. "But is he getting better?" she asked anxiously. Karl had been in school on Friday, but now that she thought of it, he had seemed a little listless for Karl.

By now there was a circle of children around her desk, and three or four tried to answer at once. Laura was assured that Karl was better if he did not get a backset.

"Well, I'm glad he is getting along as well as he is." She tried to get up to go to the blackboard. "Please—" she said. But the children were still going strong. Many accidents were being brought to light, and various illnesses.

When Betty arrived, she came thoughtfully to the desk. Since they lived

126

close to Karl's folks, she knew more. Karl had been very sick, so sick he could hardly breathe. And they had rushed him to the hospital during the night. Soberly Laura listened. "For awhile, they didn't know if Karl would live through the night," Betty added.

The children listened, wide-eyed and sober. Then one said, "My uncle had it once when he was a baby."

"I'd rather have a broke arm. Then I could run around anyway," and Rufus smiled his sweet little smile.

"Children, it is time for the bell." Laura had a smothered feeling. The children had crowded closer and closer. Several behind her seemed to be breathing down her neck. Now, as they realized she wanted to stand up, they were moving away, and she managed to stand up. Even so she stepped on Henry's toes. Henry winced and made a painful grimace.

"I'm sorry, Henry. It's a good thing you are wearing shoes."

"It didn't hurt hardly at all."

Laura took the bell and rang it vigorously outside, and the children went to their seats. All through devotions, Laura's mind kept wandering. *How frail life is. Like a slender thread that can snap in an instant.* She looked over the classroom, and suddenly the children became unutterably dear. Who was

127

to know, if this might be the last day for one of them? Or for her? The thought of Karl made her throat ache and her eyes smart. For Karl was one of her most difficult pupils, and yet he was her particular sunshine. Whenever she felt discouraged, one look at his little face, radiating such enjoyment and goodwill, was enough to brighten her day.

He was full of boundless energy and motion. Laura would explain a lesson. Karl would nod eagerly. Yes, he understood it. But after listening to her opening sentences, his mind would run to other topics. The next day in class, Karl's lesson would be done wrong.

"Do it over, Karl. Next time, listen carefully."

"You mean I'm supposed to—"

"Yes, Karl. That is what I told you yesterday."

Light would break out on Karl's face. "Oh, I see now." But the same thing happened again and again. He was usually the first one finished in his grade. Then he would sit with a gratified look on his face. To sit and study, really study, seemed impossible for Karl.

Laura remembered checking Karl's geography paper once and finding the vast continent of Asia off the tip of Florida.

For several recesses Karl and Laura had circled the globe. As they gave each continent minute attention, Karl would nod happily, "Oh, I see now. Yes, now I understand it."

"Very well," Laura had said. "Now, where is the equator?"

"Right here."

"Yes, that is the equator. Now, where is the North Pole?

"Yes, that is right." Laura had begun to relax. "And North America?"

"Right there."

"Yes, and Asia?"

"Right here."

Laura gazed unhappily at the Sahara Desert. "Don't you remember, Karl? Asia is the biggest continent."

Karl had nodded, unabashed. "Oh, I see now. Yes, now I understand it." He had given her a reassuring, happy smile.

If anyone lost a pencil or needed an eraser or forgot his lunch, Karl's heart overflowed with generosity. His face beamed if he could share with someone else.

Recalling all Karl's endearing ways made his empty desk seem even more mute and silent. *Suppose Karl never comes back.* Laura tried to get her mind on the song they were singing. It had been Henry's turn to sing and they were singing "We Are Going Down the Valley One by One." She was glad to see them sing with such good spirit. The words were meaningful—so much so that Laura felt unable to help sing. She loved to watch the children's faces as they sang. They looked so earnest and serious.

There was Dora, her brown eyes soft and serious, her conscience so tender; Susie, her eyes bright and eager, so ready to do the impossible; Rufus, singing, but absently watching Henry. Her eyes rested on Henry. He was singing with all his might, his face red with effort. Henry's voice was always heard over all the others. His was not the most musical tone, and being rather deep could not reach the high notes. But Henry had a way of drawing out his words and finishing last. There was Betty who was leaving her childhood behind and growing thoughtful and serious . . . Harvey who was so reserved and quiet that she felt she did not really know him, and yet she did know him so well. She knew that of all the children she could trust Harvey. Her eyes rested on Sally. What would Sally make of her life? Willful Sally, who needed, wise, firm guidance. Yet there were good points in Sally too . . . if one could plant in all these hearts a love for God. . . .

Somewhere ahead was death for all of them. It was something that one pushed away, and yet all must face it someday.

Laura finally concentrated as they sang the second verse.

We are going down the valley one by one,
When the labors of the weary day are

done;
One by one, the cares of life forever past,
We shall stand upon the riverbank at last.

Chapter 15

Chewing Gum

"All right, children, it is time for recess."
Laura glanced thankfully at the clock. The
whole morning had been full of interruptions. But she knew it was not so much the
interruptions that bothered her. She
watched as Sally left the room. It was Sally.
She tried to put herself in Sally's shoes.
Usually she could feel sympathetic toward
her, but this morning she was finding sympathy difficult. She had tried to favor Sally, to
let her do little things though she did not
deserve it. Sally's work showed that she was
not trying. She was getting into the old rut
again of sloppy, careless work. And her
behavior . . . something was wrong with
Sally. But what was it?

Laura sensed intuitively that Sally was
jealous of Mable and Betty. Because Mable
and Betty did good work, they could do

cetain things such as conducting extra classes with the younger students. This morning she had let Sally do the drilling with the second graders. Soon giggles and loud whispers reached her ears from the cloakroom. When Laura had gone to investigate, she saw at a glance that it would not do to leave Sally alone with a class. She wanted to give Sally a lecture. But she had the feeling that it would only drive them farther apart. "Go in to your seat," she said quietly. Sally could not have failed to hear the disappointment in Laura's voice.

The day before, Sally had been chewing gum. Thinking she might have forgotten the "no gum" rule, Laura had told her quietly to get rid of it. Now, as Laura watched her go out to play, a phrase she had read or heard went through her head. "When a child is most unloving, then he needs the most love."

But Laura's attention was brought back to the present. A small group of children were gathered around Henry's desk, and Laura saw at a glance Henry had taken it upon himself to clean out his desk. This was a major undertaking for Henry. The smaller set clustered eagerly about, ready to assist him in any way.

"If you'd keep your desk neat all the time, Henry, you wouldn't have such a mess," Laura said rather tartly. She had hoped all the children would go out. "Just look how neat Karl's desk is. And he always keeps it that way."

Karl, who was holding some books for Henry, smiled modestly, pleased and embarrassed. Henry surveyed Karl's desk. "See, everything is neat as a pin," Laura continued. "Everything has its own place— no wads of paper or untidy stacks of books. And look at Rufus's desk. His is neat too. No clutter at all."

Henry turned back to his own desk. A cluttered desk did not disturb him. He would rummage about in its depths, sometimes digging up little treasures that he had thought were lost. And desk cleaning was something of an occasion, not only for him but for the little subjects who served him.

"Don't the rest of you want to go out and play?" Laura asked hopefully. But the children shook their heads.

"We'll go if you *want* us too," said Dora sweetly. She would never, never knowingly do anything against Laura's wishes.

"I suppose you may stay and help Henry if you want too." *After all,* she thought, *they get so much pleasure out of it. Henry certainly won't get finished by himself.*

"Here, Susie, put this in the trash can." Henry was in command now. On the way to the trash can, Susie lost several wads of paper. On the way back, she met Marcus coming with more wads.

Dora happily bore away an old rag that Henry had used one day to wipe up some spilled milk.

"Who wants this pencil?" Generously, Henry held up a tiny pencil, too little to be sharpened anymore.

"I want it. No, you can have it."

"No, give it to Marcus. He wanted it first."

Marcus beamed as Henry magnanimously handed him the pencil.

Henry was in his element. He looked around the eager little circle. "Look, who wants this?" This time it was a bursted balloon. By now, everything that had been in the desk was on the floor or in somebody's arms. Henry was slightly red in the face, his hair tousled and his freckles standing out brightly.

Just then, Calvin stuck his head in the door, "Hey, why don't you all come on out and play? The sides aren't even and—"

"Hey, look what Henry gave me." Karl held up a worn-out fountain pen. "See, you put ink in here and it writes."

Interested, Calvin advanced toward the desk. "Where'd you get all that stuff?" Calvin himself was very neat. His desk was always kept in apple pie order. But there was a certain fascination about going through an untidy collection.

"Aw," Henry began, modestly. "I found some of it. I collect what I find too. See, this was in the junk. He held up a watch that no longer ran, and had no hands.

Calvin examined a few more objects interestedly. Then he said, "You all come on out." But his voice trailed away as he spied another object. Soon, the ball mitt in his hand reminded him again why he had come in. "Come on out."

But the circle around Henry barely noticed Calvin's departure. "Hey, what's this for?" Rufus held up some wire.

"It's to make a pencil holder. Shall I show you how?"

Rufus nodded eagerly.

When Laura, who had eventually gone out, came in to ring the bell, Henry and Rufus were still making the wonderful pencil holder. The other children had drifted away, and Henry's books and various items were still scattered about on the floor.

"Henry, do you mean you aren't finished with your desk?" She had forgotten all about him, and she saw with dismay that they had spent the whole recess inside. "We had such a good game of tag. I'm sorry you boys weren't out. Now do hurry and get those books in." Laura went to ring the bell.

The fresh air and exercise, coupled with the children's exuberant spirits had served as a tonic. She paused on the steps to view the countryside. The mountains were a deep purple-blue. The trees stood naked and bare.

"I wish it would snow, don't you, Teacher?" Karl paused on the steps beside her.

"Why yes, I do, Karl. But we are likely to get some soon." Laura smiled at Karl. Since he had come back, Laura kept reminding herself how frail life could be and how suddenly things could change. Karl was so thin and little and so dear. His eyes were big in his pale face.

With renewed zeal, Laura and pupils set to work. But if Laura had hoped the rest of the day would go better, she was disappointed. Looking up from a class, she noticed Sally was again chewing gum. For several minutes she sat and watched her. But Sally did not look her way. Laura finished the class and returned to her desk. She looked over the room. Most of the children were busy. The fresh air and exercise had settled their restlessness. She was glad to note that Calvin was reading a library book. Were it not for Sally, the room at the moment would be a teacher's dream.

Quietly she left the room. She stepped outside and gazed at the distant mountains. "I will lift up mine eyes unto the hills, from whence cometh my help." The verse said itself over and over in her head. "My help cometh from the LORD, which made heaven and earth." How true those words were. What was it these hills gave her? They were so mighty. But Laura could not explain why they always affected her as they did.

Alone, with the mountains before her, Laura thought and prayed. Her first impulse had been to rebuke Sally sharply before the whole room; perhaps Sally needed a public humiliation. She remembered the teacher's words. "Shaming and scolding a child publicly does not bring the kind of repentance you desire to see." But sometimes an open rebuke was necessary. Was that what Sally needed now? She tried to reason it out. Which way would draw Sally closer to God? The children would surmise that Sally had done something if she called her out of the room. Those who had seen her chewing gum would know that Sally was not getting by with disobedience. And yet, for such a little thing as chewing gum . . . but was it little? It was a deliberate act of disobedience, the breaking of a rule when she knew better. It would be easier to deal with Sally in the room. Laura imagined how it would be.

"Sally," she would say, sternly, "you are deliberately breaking one of the rules. Yesterday, I excused you when I saw you chewing gum. Today it has happened again, and now you will be punished." Yes that would be the best way, and the children would be impressed. Or was it the best way . . . for

Sally?

She thought of how Sally had been the past weeks. She remembered that she had felt she was being very longsuffering with Sally. Had she shown a condescending attitude toward Sally? Why hadn't she taken more time with her, talked to her about her work, encouraged her to do better?

As Laura gazed at the mountains, the answer came to her. In their quietness and stillness, one could feel God. Sally must feel that too. She returned to the room. She realized as she entered that some of the children had not even noticed she had been out.

Should she deal with Sally now, or wait till recess? No, it was best to go ahead now. Some of the children had been sure to see Sally. They might think Sally was getting by. Laura took a deep breath.

Some of the children had a knowing look as Sally left the room.

"Sally," Laura's voice was full of concern, "is something bothering you?"

Sally looked surprised. She had expected a lecture. "What do you mean?"

"I mean," Laura was glad Sally had lost some of her defensive attitude, "you had been trying and doing better, but lately, you have a rather I-don't-care attitude. I know," Laura went on, "sometimes we are hurt, or we are not at peace with ourselves. Something happens and we feel rebellious. And then we do things we wouldn't do otherwise. Maybe we are trying subconsciously to get even. We try to convince ourselves that it doesn't matter, or that no one cares."

Sally looked at her shoe.

"You are growing up, Sally. You have many changing thoughts and feelings, so different from what you felt at six or seven years old. Laura looked at Sally's bowed head. Sometimes she could reach the Sally inside, sometimes not.

"Sally, maybe it is my fault. Maybe I have done something that hurt you."

Sally bit her lip and looked miserable.

Finally she looked up. "It's nothing . . . well," she hesitated, "nothing much." She shrugged and looked away.

"But you don't want to tell me, Sally?"

She shook her head silently.

"Sally, if I can help you, I wish you would tell me. I think most everyone has secret cares and fears and temptations. But if we go to God with our smallest cares and fears, He will never fail us. So talk to Him, Sally. Through the day, anytime. God is always near. Talk to Him about your problems and fears, talk to Him like He was your best friend, because He is."

Laura's voice was low and earnest. "Do little things for Him. I remember when I was growing up, sometimes I wasn't sure if I really loved God. Then I read a little article about loving God. It said the more things we do for God to please Him, the more we will feel close to Him. When you go for a walk, for instance, talk to God as if He were by your side. When you are tempted to do wrong, ask Him to help you. God never fails us, but we must do our part, too. And if we really try, we have a feeling of peace, a feeling that is so much better than when we yield and give in to the little evils."

"I don't know why such a fuss is made about such little things."

Laura looked at Sally closely. Sally looked sincere, and Laura had the feeling Sally had never been taught that little things can be important.

"Haven't you heard about the boat that had a tiny leak? It was the tiny leak that caused it to sink, Sally. That's the way it is in life. The little things cause us to fall. Unless we stop and fix the leak, it will get bigger and bigger, and that little leak will cause other things to go wrong, like rotting boards, and so on. Satan does not come at first with big sins. If he can get us to do little things, then gradually we will yield to greater ones. Chewing gum doesn't seem like a big thing, but you were deliberately breaking a school rule."

"But you didn't do anything about it yesterday, so I thought you didn't care."

Laura knew she had made a mistake. She should have done more than just tell Sally to get rid of it. "I'm sorry, Sally. I imagined you had forgotten the rule. But I did tell you to get rid of it."

"I know." Sally looked down.

How different children are, Laura thought. She knew that depending on who had done the offense, one word would have been sufficient. She knew if it had been Mable, it would not have happened again. But Sally, unless she changed, would always go as far as she dared. As Laura studied Sally's face, the thought of Sally's future made her heart heavy.

"Sally, for your punishment, I'm giving you an extra assignment to do at recess. And right now I'm going to get you a Bible. I want you to read Psalm 121. Study it and look at the hills. Read it again, and try to memorize it. Somehow, my troubles have a way of resolving themselves when I stop and really look at those mountains. I think you will find it that way too. You feel so little, and God is so mighty. You can't help but feel God's love and care."

"You want me to do it right now?" Sally brushed her hand over her eyes.

"Yes, Sally. I'll bring you a Bible right now."

Would it help? Would the mountains speak to Sally, as they did to her?

But later when Laura went out to bring Sally in, Sally said quietly, hesitantly, "I'm sorry." She lifted her eyes to Laura's face and in a low voice added, "I really do want to do what is right."

Chapter 16

Losing Ground

"Yes, Christopher. Did you want to tell me something?" Laura was ready for a new day of school. She would pass out these graded papers and ring the bell. It was such a good feeling to be ready and prepared. All the assignments were made out. Everything was set for a good day. She looked at Christopher again. Gradually, Chriss was doing better. But it was a slow process. He had not cried for some time.

"Teacher, Calvin said some bad words." How little it took to change the tone of a day! For Laura, it seemed as if a cloud had suddenly crossed the sun.

"What did he say, Chriss?" Even as she looked at him, she hoped there was a mistake. But she knew that Chriss was truthful.

"I don't like to say them, Teacher, but—" he paused and looked around the room, "I'll whisper them to you."

She heard the whispered words and her heart sank. "When did you hear him, Chriss?"

"It was yesterday on the way home and this morning when we came. And, Teacher, he has a dirty book too."

"A dirty book?"

"Yes, Mable saw it too."

Chriss, you won't ever repeat those words, will you?" Laura knew as she gazed at Chriss that she did love him very much. There was something about his timid face, looking at her so earnestly. And she was glad he had been shocked by the words he had heard. Even though his mother babied him, he had been taught about right and wrong.

All the other children were outside, and after Chriss had gone, Laura went to Calvin's desk and searched, but she found nothing. His desk was neat, everything in place. A lump came to her throat, and she walked to the window and looked out.

Calvin had been doing better. She had started giving him odd jobs to do when he was finished with his work. And she had found that Calvin worked as he played—with all his might. The first time, she had sent him out to sweep the closet. All the while he was at it, she was dimly conscious of banging sounds and noises. Finally, when she was convinced he was up to mischief—for it did not take that long to sweep the closet—she had gone to investigate. She had found him moving everything from the closet to the outside. She tried not to look surprised. "Nearly done?" she had asked casually.

"I've still got this part to do." He waved his hand over some boxes that were yet to be moved. His face was flushed, and a cobweb hung in his hair. "I have the top part clean now."

She nodded, relieved. "You are doing a good job, I see."

So now, whenever Calvin had his work finished, he sat and watched her expectantly. If she did not notice, he soon raised his hand. And she found that she could always trust him to do the job right. And he was quieter. If she did not have something lined up for him to do, he would settle down with a book.

A dirty book, Chriss had said—bad words and a dirty book. Chriss had said Mable had seen it too. She would talk with Mable.

At first Mable was hesitant. But when she saw how concerned Laura was and that no blame rested on her, she told all she knew. She had not heard Calvin say any words, but Chriss had, and she had seen the book in his desk.

After Laura had talked with Mable, she tried to gather herself together. She knew she must talk to Calvin. But just then it

146

seemed like one of the hardest things she had ever faced.

But Calvin did not own up to the bad words. He gazed stony-faced at the wall. Nor did he seem to know anything about a comic book.

"Calvin, please tell me the truth. Lying makes it so much worse."

Calvin looked at his teacher. He looked away. "Somebody is trying to get me in trouble."

And Laura began to hope. *Perhaps Chriss misunderstood . . . but the comic book. . . .* She took a deep breath. It was past time to begin school. She could not punish Calvin now. If there had been two who had heard him say the words, it would be different, but it was Calvin's word against Chriss's. As for the comic book, she had found nothing of it either. Heavyhearted, she dismissed Calvin.

It was a long day. Laura found it hard to concentrate on the lessons. In the back of her mind, she knew she must do something, but what?

After the children had gone home, she tried to decide. She wavered between two choices. She could let the whole thing drop—if there was any truth in what Chriss had said, sooner or later, Calvin would be found out.

The other alternative was to get in contact with Calvin's parents. She knew somehow

147

that this was what she must do. But she shrank from it. She had seen Calvin's folks, but although they were friendly, they had never taken time to ask about Calvin. *Maybe they will take his part. Maybe* . . . she tried to push the thoughts away. She knew if she stayed late enough, Calvin's father would be passing the school on his way home from work. Yes, she knew that was what she must do She would stop him and talk with him then.

Later that evening, Laura thought over her encounter with Calvin's father. It had been very brief. She had told him the charges that had come against Calvin and that Calvin had denied them. The man did not show surprise. He was very matter-of-fact about it. "I'll talk with the boy and let you know one way or the other in the morning."

The next morning when Laura got to school, there was a note on her desk. Quickly she picked it up. Eagerly, yet dreading too, she tore it open. "Dear Teacher," she read, "Calvin says he did say some words he shouldn't have. You punish him as you think." It was signed by Calvin's father.

She took a deep breath. So Calvin had confessed. But why had he lied to her? There was no mention made of a comic book. Had his father forgotten about that? And now she must punish him. For some reason, she felt disappointed though she could not say exactly why. She remembered how very concerned some of the other parents were when their children misbehaved.

As Laura passed through the cloakroom to call Calvin in, she saw his coat hanging there. On impulse, she took it off the hook and looked into the pocket. Something was there. She pulled it out, and her shocked gaze saw the book that Mable had told her about. She opened the cover and her eyes fell on a lewd picture. *A book like that! A book like that in school! Please God, help me,* she prayed silently.

Mechanically, she called Calvin in. He was looking sullen and would not look at Laura. Laura swallowed. It had seemed as if she and Calvin had been climbing the mountain together. But now the little victories along the way seemed lost.

And now also the enormity of her position swept over her. There was Calvin with his restless energy, his eager questing mind, still a child, but growing up . . . Calvin who loved adventure and excitement, ready for anything new, anything different . . . Calvin who was so full of badness, and yet so much goodness . . . Calvin looking at such a book!

"Calvin," she said, finally, when she could speak, "where did you get this book?"

"I found it." Calvin did not look up. "It was," he paused, "it was lying in the ditch."

"Why didn't you tell me yesterday, Calvin? Why did you lie to me?"

Calvin did not answer.

"Calvin, you know what happens to liars. The Bible says that all liars will have their place in the lake that burns with fire and brimstone. And it won't be for a hundred years or a thousand—that would be a long, long time, but it will be forever and ever!" She looked at him as he stood there. He would not look at her. There was a miserable look on his face, and yet a certain amount of defiance. As usual, he was dressed neatly. Calvin never came to school dirty or dressed slovenly.

She looked at the comic book. There was nothing comic about it. "Calvin," Laura's voice was strong with feeling, "books like this are worse than poison. They stain your mind. You don't know and I don't know how wicked they are."

Calvin looked up. The intensity of Laura's voice compelled him to look at her. Then he spoke. "I've seen Dad look at funnies in a comic book."

Laura clasped her hands, remembering Calvin had once said his father got angry too. What kind of a man was Calvin's father?

"Did you tell your father last night you have this book?"

"Well, not exactly. He asked if I had one." Calvin hesitated.

"What did you tell him, Calvin?"

"I told him I found one once."

"And what did he tell you to do?"

"He said I'd better get rid of it."

"But he didn't see it?"

"No. Dad thinks some of them are funny."

What should she say? Surely Calvin's father had no idea what kind of comic book Calvin had. And why hadn't he searched himself? Why didn't he tell his son why such things were wrong?

"Look, Calvin, some comic books are nothing but that—funny, that's all. But if the devil can get us to read them, that is just what he wants us to do. He wants to fill up our mind with silly, empty stuff. That way he can keep us from having good, worthwhile thoughts. Then, when we read those, he will come with books that are not fit for anyone to read. He knows if we take time to read the funnies, he can more easily get us to read these filthy ones." She picked up the book and tore it to bits.

Calvin watched silently. Laura put the torn book into a bag. "I won't even put it in the trash can, Calvin. When we are through, we'll take it out and burn it." She turned to him again. "Calvin, you don't ever come to school dirty, do you?"

"Of course not, Teacher." He looked at her, puzzled.

"I know you don't, Calvin. You are clean

and neat, and that is right. But don't you want to be just as clean on the inside? See, saying bad words, reading trash, all that makes your mind dirty. You want to grow up strong. But lies and bad words and dirty books make you weak on the inside. You can't grow strong and straight. You are crippled on the inside, and then when Satan comes with the big temptations, do you know what happens? You are too weak and crippled, too dirty to stand up and do what is right. Do you understand, Calvin?"

The boy nodded slowly.

"You know I must punish you, Calvin." Laura turned away, her eyes blinded by tears. Never had this duty appeared so hard to do as it did then.

Calvin nodded. He submitted quietly to his punishment.

Chapter 17

The Director Comes Again

Christmas had come and gone. It had been a happy season for them all. The New Year was past, and Laura realized they were in the mid-year slump.

She had rejoiced with the children when the first snow had come. Falling snow always put her in a quiet, awed mood. It affected the children too. Laura felt she would never forget the first snow she had shared with a roomful of children. They had been bending over their lessons until someone spied the flakes falling lazily to the ground. "Snow! Snow!" They breathed the magic words as loud as they could. And with the breathing of that word, the whole room changed from dull, everyday work to wonder and delight.

But it did not put them in a quiet, awed mood! The children could hardly contain themselves. Calvin gave a whistle of amazement. The small children clapped their hands, and Rufus—quiet, timid Rufus— stood up on his seat to have a better view.

"Okay, you may all go to the window for a good look." As one man they rose and made for the windows. "Quiet, please! Don't push." But Laura had the feeling she was talking to the wall.

"Oh, just look at it come down!"

"We can go sledding on the hill!"

"I hope it snows *this high!*" Henry lifted his hand high above his head.

"I hope it snows that high!" said another, waving his arms to show enormous heights.

"Now since you have had a look, you may return to your seats." They turned slowly, reluctantly away, each one trying to be the last to leave the window. They took last looks, then another last look, as if never expecting to see the snow fall again.

They went to their desks, but the spell of the first snow was upon them. There was some pretense made of study, but even Laura found it hard to keep her eyes from wandering out the window. And then as the snow began to fall thick and fast, Laura felt quite helpless. The children were in such glee, such a state of excitement, that she felt she must laugh herself. Happily, they blundered through their lessons.

When recess came, Laura had the feeling that if she did not dismiss immediately, the room would burst. Today there was no question of staying in. The children donned their wraps with amazing speed and tumbled out the door. Laura walked to the window and looked out. Had God, in His wisdom, known what enjoyment children would get out of snow? He could have created things differently, but He had made everything in the most wonderful way.

After the first snow, there had been more. And there were wet gloves and boots to contend with, tracked floors and lost mittens.

This morning as Laura looked about the room, she was impressed with the emptiness of it, and yet it seemed to talk. Each desk spoke silently, but eloquently of its owner. There was a charm in that early morning hour when she was alone, yet not alone, in the empty schoolroom. There in the presence of the desks she would kneel first and pray. Now and then a board creaked. There was the call of the cardinal, the scolding of a blue jay, and the quiet of the morning. It was her golden hour, and she loved it.

The hills this morning were a misty blue. They looked distant, aloof in their grandeur, so different from the warm bue and purple shades they had worn in the autumn. Reluctantly Laura turned from the window. It would not do to gaze out the window too long. There was always so much to do. If only she could think of something to break up the monotony of the school days. The children seemed bored. She glanced at the bulletin board. That was something. It needed to be changed. And they all enjoyed working on that.

She looked up sometime later to see Henry coming. Several steps behind him was Walter. Walter was seldom in a hurry. But she could see by the way Henry walked he had news again.

As soon as he had taken off his wraps, he hastened into the room. "Good morning, Henry. Any special news this morning?"

"Good morning, Teacher." Henry had time for a greeting this morning. He paused meaningfully. Then he said, "Calvin didn't come today."

"Well, I wonder why?" She frowned a little. "Is he sick."

"It's hard telling. Mom said the flu is around, and it is awful catching." The door opened and several children hurried up. They did not want to miss anything.

"What's wrong, Henry? What's catching?"

"Mom said the flu." Henry looked down with dignity. He had a certain air, as if the smaller children were too little to be in on this. Then in an undertone to Laura, he asked, "What are you going to do about Calvin?"

Laura had a strong desire to laugh. "Well,

we'll wait till tomorrow to have that English test. Maybe he will be here by then."

Henry nodded. "He might be."

So. A whole day without Calvin in it. The day would be quiet. It was so hard to keep him busy and occupied. These winter days were boring to Calvin. Of course, she was sorry if he was sick.

When Laura rang the bell, she was surprised how much quieter the children were. But then, Calvin made enough noise and commotion for several children. Still, there was an emptiness in the room, an emptiness she was conscious of all day. The day lacked flavor. But Laura was not about to admit that she missed Calvin with all his noise and mischief.

That afternoon the School Director stopped in. They were pleased with her teaching, he said, and they hoped she would consider another term with them. He paused and Laura remembered her earlier resolution. It was surprising how many thoughts could troop through your mind in only a few moments. Another year with Calvin in it? Today she had felt quite calm, relaxed, and competent—the way she had always thought a teacher should feel. In another school, she could start over, make a fresh beginning. She would not let herself get so emotionally involved. It would be terribly hard to leave, but Calvin needed a teacher who was steady and even-tempered, one who was wise and firm and gentle.

She shook her head. She opened her mouth to say that she had considered already, but the Director waved his hand. "No, no. Don't give your answer now. You need time to think it over. Hasty decisions are not good. You should take time to think and pray over something like this."

She knew it was true. But she had wanted to give her answer now, before she changed her mind. She did not like times of indecision, when she was not sure if she was trying to do what *she* wanted to do, or what God wanted her to do.

"I'll come back in a few weeks," the Director was saying. He glanced around for a calendar. "Take your time."

Laura went back to her work, but she found herself staring at the mountains. The peace she had felt that morning was gone. There was an inward jarring, a note of discord. *What is wrong?* she asked herself. *Surely it is not wrong to teach at some other place. Teaching is a worthwhile work, and they can find someone else to take my place here.* She would let the Director know as soon as she saw him again. That would give them plenty of time to look for someone else. It would be better for her and Calvin both.

The next morning Calvin's father drove in with Calvin. They were the first to come, and Calvin's father stepped into the school-room.

"Hello." He glanced around the room. "I've been meaning to stop in, but seems like there's always something else a-going." He paused. "How is Calvin doing?"

Laura hesitated. She had often longed for just such a time as this to talk to Calvin's parents. But it was a different matter with Calvin standing there, hearing every word. She wished his father would tell him to go to the cloakroom or someplace else while they talked. How could she tell his father what a problem Calvin was with Calvin standing right there? "He is doing good work as a rule," she heard herself say.

"Well, he can do good work if he wants to. But I know he is a bad boy. Gets in all kinds of mischief." The man's voice was matter-of-fact, as if Calvin's badness were something that could not be helped. "We are hoping he will outgrow it." Laura glanced at Calvin. He was looking at his shoes. She must say something. She must stop the words from coming. To be told that you are bad . . . no wonder Calvin acted as he did. But his father's voice was not unkind. He was merely saying how things were. "Does he act up a lot, here in school?" he was asking.

It seemed as if time stood still. As if even the clock were waiting to see what she would say. She was conscious of Calvin standing there, waiting to be condemned by his teacher, waiting miserably to hear all the grievances and problems she had had with him. And Laura, glancing at his face, could see he was trying hard to look indifferent, aloof, as if it didn't matter. But she saw the look in his eyes.

"He is," she paused. She must be honest. "He is a very normal boy," she heard herself say. "And he tries. That is the important thing, isn't it?" That was true, he did try. Of course, she could not see how hard he tried sometimes. The man was still standing there as if expecting her to say more. "We fail too sometimes with children. They have so much growing up to do. It takes a lot of patience and prayer and guidance, doesn't it?" She stopped, wondering why she had said so much and not sure of what she really had said.

"Yes," Calvin's father nodded. "That's right. Well, you'll just have to punish him when you need to." He turned to go. "Now, Calvin, don't you walk home. You stay here until someone comes to pick you up." He turned back to Laura. "He hurt his ankle yesterday. The doctor said he's to stay off it as much as he can." He gave Calvin a pat on the back as he left.

Laura watched him leave. She felt perplexed and not a little anxious. How could Calvin's father expect him to behave, if they, his parents, took for granted he was bad? Children usually live up to their parents' expectations. *What is the use of being good if your own parents are convinced you are bad?* Laura did not like even the sound of the word *bad*. Everyone is born with a sinful nature, but to say those things to a child in such a way! She looked up the word in a dictionary. *Bad:* "evil, wicked, vicious, naughty, incompetent; poor, valueless." Laura closed the dictionary with a snap. *Valueless!* She was suddenly blinking back tears. What parent would call his child valueless? Or any of the other words?

She remembered those first trying weeks of school when Calvin had been such a problem, when she had talked and prodded and punished and Calvin had been so indifferent, staring at the wall or out the window when she admonished him. And he had seemed to have no incentive at all to do better. But why should he try to do better if it was expected of him to be bad?

And that day, Laura saw how good Calvin could be. He was quiet and well-behaved, with a certain humbleness in his manner that she had never seen in Calvin before.

Chapter 18

Truth Is Courage

Laura had wished for something to break the monotony of the school days, but she would not, certainly not, have chosen Calvin to be the one to do it! Those first days Calvin had been almost painfully good. Because of his ankle, he could not go out to play, so he spent the whole day in the schoolhouse. Having no way of releasing his restless, pent-up energy, he took it out on the ones who stayed inside. He stood behind the door and growled at the little ones when they came in or out. He hobbled after Susie, who screamed in delighted dread as he tried to grab her foot.

"Calvin, your father said you are supposed to keep quiet."

Calvin grinned. His dark eyes had a teasing light in them. He could tell when Laura was about to laugh and did not want to.

When she stepped out of the room he crawled under her desk.

"Shh, don't tell," he hissed to the wide-eyed little girls. When Laura returned, the room was unusually quiet.

"Where is Calvin?" she asked, suddenly suspicious. The little girls giggled. Laura looked around the room. Everything appeared as usual. The fire in the stove was crackling pleasantly and gave the room a homey, cozy air. Calvin could not disappear into thin air. Cautiously, she approached her desk, and as she sat down, something grabbed her foot.

"Now, Calvin," she tried to sound stern. He crawled out, grinning. There was a teasing look in his dark eyes. And looking at Calvin, Laura again found it hard to look sober. It would have been so easy in that moment to laugh and do something amusing in return. But she was a teacher, she told herself. And she knew that a teacher must be a friend but keep a certain amount of dignity as well.

"I think you need some work to do," she said. "Why don't you read a book?"

Calvin shrugged. He did not like to read a book. Not at recess.

"Here's a puzzle, Calvin. Why don't we start putting this together?" Calvin looked politely at the puzzle, but it offered no action.

The little girls came up to the table. "We'll help. May we, Teacher?"

"Of course. The more that help, the faster it will get finished." Laura dumped out the pieces on the table and everyone was soon busy.

Not until during the next class period did Laura notice something was wrong with Henry. She was looking at Sally. She had not had to punish Sally since the day she had left her on the steps to study the psalm and look at the mountains. There had been little things, but a few words had been sufficient. Now, Sally looked up and smiled, and Laura felt as though she had received a gift. A smile from Sally! It meant somehow that Sally trusted her.

And then Henry sighed. It was such a deep, long, heartfelt sigh that it arrested Laura's attention. There was that in Henry's face and manner that gave her the feeling Henry was loaded down with cares and burdens too great for even his sturdy shoulders. She watched him closely.

"Yes, George?" Laura momentarily forgot Henry as she saw George waving his hand in a desperate fashion. Just then he gave a loud hiccough. He was trying to suppress them from coming, but it was impossible. As another burst from him, some of the children giggled. "Go get a drink," she said, nodding to George.

She looked at Henry again. Even his freckles seemed to cry out for sympathy, dotting his face like so many pinpoints of woe.

"What is your trouble, Henry?"

Usually Henry was self-reliant, steady, and cheerful in adversity. He seemed to move on, undaunted by the little trials that came up in school life and discouraged the others. He would plod on, unmoved even by such things as poor grades. If he had to do work over, he did it over. That was all a part of life. But now, big tears were welling up in Henry's eyes. For a moment, he did not speak. When his voice came out, there was, Laura detected, a slight quiver in it.

"I can't get this problem." He looked down at his paper.

Laura hastened to his side. In teaching, she had found, one must be something of a sleuth. Children are honest. But sometimes they say one thing when they really need something else. It was most unlike Henry to cry over a problem.

"How many problems do you still have to do?" she asked in a low voice. The other children eyed Henry meditatively. Reluctantly, they returned to their books as they saw nothing unusual developing.

"Well," Laura's voice was brisk. She must not sound too sympathetic or Henry might cry. "If you keep busy, you'll get done."

"But I don't have my lesson finished from yesterday."

Well. That was serious. But she must not scold him now.

"And my head hurts," Henry finished.

Now Laura knew. "Henry," she said softly, "go out to the broom closet."

Henry rose obediently and marched out, as a soldier might to his fate. He knew as well as anyone what lay in the broom closet. Yet the teacher's voice had been kind. . . .

The children, as one man, looked up. They had quite forgotten about Henry, except a few idle ones, including Calvin, who had been contenting himself by making faces at the smallest children. He could pull his face into terrible contortions and grimaces. The little ones looked upon him with awe, admiration, and disapproval. As Laura followed Henry, she glanced at Dora. She was looking at Calvin with fascinated yet disapproving eyes. Laura caught Calvin's eye and shook her head. She knew, Calvin had an attraction about him. There was something about his black hair and the light in his dark eyes and just the whole character that was Calvin.

Henry was in the closet. He was visibly shaken, but he was trying to be brave. He knew that handing in late papers was little short of a crime. Laura looked at him closely, and he dropped his eyes. Never had he looked so miserable in school.

"Henry, how did you feel this morning?"

Henry's mouth dropped open. It was a funny way to begin a punishment. "I don't remember. Well, I didn't eat much. I wasn't hungry."

Laura felt his forehead. "Henry, I believe you are running a temperature. You feel hot. Where you really should be is in bed."

Henry's tears spilled over. He could have taken his punishment without a whimper, but his teacher's sympathy and the sudden turn of events were too much.

"Don't cry, Henry." Laura sounded suddenly very businesslike. "I'll send someone over to the neighbors for some medicine, and you can lie down. Do you feel awfully bad?"

"No, Teacher. I think I feel a bit better."

"I'm glad to hear that." She made him as comfortable as possible. He soon regained his cheerfulness, and as Laura returned to the room, a pang went through her. Next year, she would not be here to do anything for Henry—Henry, who was so solid and good-natured and reliable, who kept her posted on all the neighborhood news. She gave a little sigh.

Through the day, she felt quite settled in her mind. It would be better for her to find another school. But at night she would wake up, and the inward peace was missing. She had instead a dissatisfied, doubtful feeling. She told herself it was because she would miss the children.

The next morning as Laura was paging through one of her devotional books, her eyes fell on a paragraph written by George Eliot.

We mustn't be in a hurry to fix and choose our own lot; we must wait to be guided. We are led on, like the little children, by a way that we know not. It is a vain thought to flee from the work that God appoints us, for the sake of finding a greater blessing to our own souls; as if we could choose for ourselves where we shall find the fulness of the Divine Presence, instead of seeking it where alone it is to be found, in loving obedience.

In loving obedience . . . she read the words again. *Led on by a way that we know not.* . . . She closed the book. The fleeting thought came to her that God had a purpose in this. Was He leading her on, here in this school, by a way that she knew not? Was she choosing her own way, running from the work God had given her to do?

But I cannot cope with Calvin, she told herself. *Lying, bad words, bad books, all the trouble I have had with him—next term, Calvin will be older and surely that much harder to manage.*

And so she was pulled first one way and then another, sure in her own mind that she did not want to teach here again, yet feeling she was "fleeing the work that God had appointed to her."

The days following, Laura felt cross and edgy. And the mountains, as she gazed at them now, made her feel only more troubled. They rebuked her in their silent majesty.

Nor did it help matters any to have Calvin still in the schoolhouse. He prowled about restlessly at recess. When one of the girls turned her back, he unraveled her knitting. Laura sent him to his desk, and Calvin could tell by her tone of voice that this time she was not smiling inside. He slunk to his seat under a battery of cold stares from the girls. As he sat in his desk, his face grew darker by the minute.

Laura felt a pang of remorse. She knew that Calvin needed some diversion too. Usually he could persuade one or two of the boys to stay in with him. But today they had brought their kites, and every one of them had trooped out with gay abandon. He scowled at the girls, and shortly later was seeing how far he could tip his desk without turning it over.

"Calvin."

He looked up to see Laura standing beside him. "I'll play a game of checkers with you."

He had to grin. "Aw, you don't have to."

"I want to, Calvin."

It became an engrossing game. Halfway through the game, Karl came in. He smiled apologetically as he desposited a small wrapped parcel on Laura's desk. "Mom said I can give you *that*."

"Thank you, Karl. But you didn't come in just to give me that, did you?"

"Well," there was still apology on his face, sorry that he must interrupt her like this. "I thought I'd bring it in while I was thinking about it." He smiled and hurried out again.

Laura felt very humble. He could have given it at noon when he opened his lunch box anyway. Karl was so little and thin. At times a fear shot through her that Karl might not gain back his health. *And whatever would I do without Karl?* She swallowed the lump that came to her throat.

"It's your move, Teacher."

"Is it?" Laura looked down at the checkerboard. Calvin was a shrewd player.

"That was a good game, wasn't it," he said as they finished.

"Well, I guess you think so since you beat." She laughed as she rose from her seat to get the bell.

"Teacher." Calvin came up to her desk. He glanced at the girls to see if they were noticing. "I wanted to tell you I, I—" he stammered and stopped.

"What did you want to say, Calvin?" Laura asked kindly.

"Well, I didn't exactly say the truth this morning and then a bad word slipped out."

"Oh, I see. I am so glad you told me. Who were you talking with?"

"Henry and me was talking. And I was mad because I couldn't fly my kite. I don't know if Henry heard the words or not."

"I'm so very glad you told me." Laura swallowed and tears stung her eyes. "You, you have won a victory, Calvin, by coming and confessing. Now we want to do something to help you overcome this."

"Maybe I could write that saying again."

"Saying?"

"You know. 'Falsehood is cowardice; truth is courage.'"

"Oh yes." So he had remembered! "Yes, that would be fitting."

That night Laura could not sleep. The wise saying that she had told Calvin she hoped he would always remember kept going through her head. "Falsehood is cowardice; truth is courage." And Calvin had remembered. She was the one who had forgotten. *Truth is courage.* Was she being true to herself, true to her duty, if she left this school for another? She had told herself she was leaving because of Calvin—mostly. But in the darkness she knew it was like running away. She was running away because she was afraid she could not handle Calvin—Calvin with all his charm, his restless energy, his keen mind, his eagerness for anything new and different . . . Calvin with parents who were too permissive. What was going to happen to Calvin?

And she would leave because she was afraid. But the burden on her heart would not go away. The fear she had for Calvin, coupled with her own wavering mind, made her miserable. She was pulled one way and then another. She remembered how Calvin had come and whispered his confession to her. *Falsehood is cowardice.* The words rang in her mind. Was she being false to her duty, a coward, because she could not face the duty that lay before her?

It was very late before she fell into a troubled sleep.

Chapter 19

The Hills at Peace

"Yes, Dora, did you want to tell me something?"

Dora's eyes were big and worried. "Teacher," and she drew closer to Laura. "Teacher, the book said, 'Do not look back,' but I looked back. Did I cheat?" By now, Dora's tears had spilled over and she sobbed brokenly.

Laura was touched. She put her arm around the sobbing girl. She thought of Dora's young mother. She left no stone unturned to have her little girl do her best in school. And Dora's mother was not the only concerned parent. There were many who came and asked how their children were doing. Laura often wondered if they had any idea how much it meant to her, knowing they were standing behind her, supporting her, despite her own faults and failures.

And there was no one like Dora. Dora would be standing at the trash can peeling an orange, most of the other children having gone out to play.

"You have a nice orange, Dora."

"It isn't mine."

"Oh, are you peeling it for someone?"

"Yes, Susie couldn't start it." Carefully she peeled the whole orange and gave it to Susie.

Another time, Dora had asked, "Teacher, may Cathy and I trade places?"

"Why do you want to trade, Dora?"

"Well, Cathy does not like to sit in the back."

"Don't you mind moving, Dora? Do you really want to sit in the back?"

"Oh, it doesn't matter. I can sit in the back." Dora was so sweet and unselfish that sometimes Laura hardly knew what to do with her.

Now as she looked at the weeping girl, she knew she should have made it more clear to the children how to do the page. "I expected you to look back, because the words were new. The next time we do them, I will expect you not to look back. But I will tell you. I am glad you do not want to cheat."

Dora tried to stop crying.

"Don't feel bad, Dora. See it was my fault too. Usually we go over the lesson together, but today we didn't." By the time she had finished talking, Dora was smiling again.

That whole day seemed destined to be full of blunders. And Laura knew the fault lay within herself. All the things she had been trying to teach the children came to her mind at startling moments. Although she tried to convince herself that it was right to leave this school, she knew deep down that she had lost her peace, the peace she had told Sally about. Through the day, she could convince herself, but at night in the darkness, she faced the real truth. There the children pulled and wrenched at her heart.

She expected the Director to stop in any day and she knew she must have her answer ready.

She caught herself snapping at the children. Then filled with remorse, she tried to be extra kind. Calvin's ankle was better, but he seemed to be the very embodiment of mischief. Even good-natured Henry seemed to have turned against all that stood for quiet, peace, and order.

"Calvin, bring me that rubber band." Laura's voice was sharp. Calvin rose reluctantly. He glanced at Henry, but without a word he came up and put it on the desk. Laura picked it up and dropped it into her drawer. The children were exchanging glances. She had the feeling that everyone was turning against her. She took a deep breath. She had a strong desire to cry. She rose suddenly, walked to the window and looked out. The hills were breathtaking in color. The sun reflected on them, making some parts a deep purple-blue, while others in the shadow looked soft and misty. But looking at them now brought no comfort. They only tended to make her feel more miserable inside. *They* were so calm and grand, so peaceful in their glory, so settled in the place God had given them. She turned away. She was glad to see that it was time for recess.

As the children filed out, Henry came up to her desk. "Teacher, that was my rubber band."

"Why did Calvin have it?" Laura's voice was still sharp, and Henry paled slightly.

But Henry was not a coward. "I snapped it and it landed beside him." Henry looked down. His freckles dotted his face in embarrassment.

"Well, Henry, I'm *very* disappointed." As soon as she had said the words, she knew she should have commended Henry for coming and confessing. And the thought occured to her that Calvin could have come and cleared himself. Her back had been turned, but she had looked around just in time to see Calvin pick it up beside his desk. She knew a rubber band could do a lot of things in Calvin's hands, and she had assumed he had been snapping it. But in her present unhappy frame of mind, she did not feel like praising Henry for his truthfulness either.

"I don't want to let it happen again." Henry looked very serious.

"Well, I hope not." Laura bit her lip. Why was she so sharp and unfeeling? Henry's face smote her.

"Do you want me to stay in?" Henry asked. Now, he could meet his teacher's eyes again. Staunchly he waited to hear his sentence.

Laura looked down. Because she was unhappy herself, did she have to take it out on the children? It was not their fault she was at odds with herself. And now Henry was asking about a punishment. She looked at him reflectively. "No, Henry. Because you were so honest and came and told me this, I won't give you a punishment . . . this time." She glanced around the room. Everyone was outside. Henry nodded and smiled, and suddenly his freckles looked cheerful again.

Laura followed Henry outside. Most of the boys had gone to the far end of the ball diamond to watch some loggers who were moving into the woods. As she stood watching, she could see that the boys kept watching in her direction, and then a figure detached itself from the others. As he came closer, she saw it was Calvin. Was he sick? Had something happened? He kept glancing back, as though afraid he would miss something.

"Teacher, did you want something?" he asked as he approached her.

"I—" Laura was taken aback. Had Calvin come up just because he thought she had wanted something?

"I thought maybe you wanted something."

"No, Calvin." She felt speechless. What could she say? And he had come all the way for nothing. "But, Calvin, you can tell the boys I'm giving you some extra recess," she said impulsively. "And, Calvin, Henry told me that was his rubber band. I'm glad you were not snapping it."

"Aw . . ." Calvin looked down. "But I was going to." He grinned suddenly. "How much recess did you say?"

"I didn't say, but I'll ring when I want you to come." She turned and went to join the girls. The children had not had any extra recess for a good while, and watching the loggers would be an interesting experience for them.

That afternoon the Director stopped in. He frowned worriedly. "Are you still having trouble with Calvin?"

"Not more so than usual." Laura felt a little puzzled. She had expected the Director would ask her what her plans were.

The Director scratched his head. "Then you feel he is making an improvement?"

Laura hesitated. Was Calvin improving?

His goodness and badness were so mixed up that he left her baffled. When she wanted to punish him, she found herself weakening because he was sure to turn around and do something that left her feeling humbled and unsure of herself.

"Well, you don't need to answer if you don't want to," the Director spoke again, looking more worried still. "From the time he has entered school, we have had a problem there. I had hoped as the boy grew older, it would change for the better. And he has been making trouble all year."

"Yes—" Laura faltered.

"There is little hope of improvement next year, is there? Unless his parents. . . ." The Director sighed and shook his head. He did not finish his sentence, but Laura knew. Calvin needed firm but loving upbringing. He needed to know that he had good qualities, that he was not all bad. She thought of how he had been those first trying weeks of school.

"He has improved though. He does try." Had he not come and confessed? "Really, there is so much good in Calvin. If only it can be brought out. Once you know him, you are surprised at what good qualities he has." She had to defend him, though she could not have told why. She rememberd suddenly how he had tagged George out, how he had voluntarily told her about saying a bad word, and how he had come up from the playground that day to see if she had wanted something. Calvin, the boy who used to avoid her . . . a lump came into her throat.

"Well, I am glad to hear that. All his teachers so far had a lot of complaints about him. But the boy cannot be blamed. The training of children starts in the home."

"Yes, that is true." Laura looked at her hands. She longed to say that Calvin had improved on all points, but then she remembered the time she had found the book in his coat pocket. Whenever she was almost convinced that now he was a better boy, something happened to destroy that hope. "But he doesn't lie to me, as he did at first," she said suddenly. "Of course, I don't know how soon he may do it again. And he does try to control his temper."

"That is good. Calvin needs an understanding teacher. There is more than an education needed when one teaches children."

"Yes," Laura murmured. She tried to brush the mist from her eyes. She had been so sure that Calvin needed another teacher. A wise, calm teacher, a teacher who always thought before she spoke. She was quick-spoken and hasty, too emotional. Of all teachers, she was the most unfitted. Then the thought came to her that God had seen that she needed a pupil like Calvin. She had been "led by a way she knew not." With her good children, she had no struggles. It was not hard to control her tongue with Dora or Henry, but with the difficult ones she had wrestled and cried and prayed.

"I should look at the attendance records," the Director broke into her thoughts.

After he had examined them, he said, "Well, I see they are in good order.

"And have you decided what you want to do?"

"Yes, I have decided." She had not known until that moment, and she was surprised at herself. To have someone else come in and take her place, someone who might not understand Calvin, someone who would not know how good he could be . . . or how bad, someone else to take her place with Dora and Susie . . . those good and problem children all mixed up in a wonderful way. . . . Oh, they were *hers* to cry for and wrestle over and pray for, *hers* to laugh, work, and play with.

"I want to teach here, again, if I may." She knew she did not want to be free of this burden of caring. She knew another year would bring its heartaches and joys. But God would still be God. She must be true to herself and true to her duty.

The inward jarring was gone, she could feel peace and quiet within. *Truth is courage*, she told herself. And when one is true,

181

then there is peace.

In the distance, the mountains seemed to reach to the very heavens. So tall, so majestic in their mighty grandeur! They stood like silent but glorious sentinels that had watched over them all—so silent, yet so eloquent in speaking of the Almighty God! They seemed now to echo with the beauty of peace.